WORCESTERSHIRE SALT

A History of Stoke Prior Salt Works

by

Alan White

hb Halfshire Books

Halfshire Books
6 High Street, Bromsgrove
Worcestershire B61 8HQ

First published in Great Britain
by Halfshire Books 1996

Copyright © Alan White

ISBN 1 899062 01 7

All rights reserved. No part of this publication may be reproduced, stored in a retrieval system, or transmitted in any form or by any means, electronic, mechanical, photocopying, recording or otherwise, without the prior permission of the publishers.

Typeset/Designed in New Century Schoolbook by
Avonset, St Chads Green, Midsomer Norton, near Bath BA3 2JT
Printed in Great Britain by The Looseleaf Company, Bowerhill, Melksham

Contents

List of illustrations	v
Stoke Works: notable dates	vii
Weights and measures	viii
Introduction and memories of Stoke Works	1
Chapter 1 **The pre-Corbett era: 1825-52**	7
Beginnings on the west side of the canal	7
Jonathan Fardon's works on the east side of the canal	9
Progress on the west side of the canal	12
Fardon and Gossage's works	13
The British Alkali Company	16
The Imperial Salt and Alkali Company	20
Arrival of the Birmingham and Gloucester Railway	20
Problems in the 1840s and their consequences	22
Jonathan Fardon	26
Chapter 2 **The Corbett era: 1852-89**	29
Takeover of the Stoke Works by John Corbett	29
Corbett's marriage and family	35
Corbett's Stoke Prior Salt Works	37
Corbett's boatyard, canal boats, and use of railways	39
Ending of female labour in the salt works	42
Corbett's provisions for, and expecations of, his employees	44
Travels and awards	49
Public figure and benefactor	49
The Chateau Impney and Corbett's marriage breakdown	50
Works management and performance	52
Events leading to the Salt Union takeover	53

Chapter 3	**Under the Salt Union and ICI: 1889-1972**	55
	John Corbett and the Salt Union, 1889-94	55
	William Young's management, 1894-1910	56
	Harry Lockhead's management, 1910-30	58
	Later works managers	60
	Salt production under the Salt Union	62
	World War Two and the end of salt carrying by canal	67
	The ICI vacuum plant	70
	End of open-pan salt production	77
	Demise of the works railways and rail transport	78
	Closure of the works	80
Appendices	A: Apprenticeship indenture, 1869	82
	B: 'George's Ghost'	84
	C: Stoke Works village	85
Some documentary sources		87

List of illustrations

Photographs

Aerial photograph of Stoke Works taken around 1920	19
Aerial photograph taken after 1924 when the big chimney was truncated	19
Three views of the works from the brine reservoir	25
The works' fire brigade and old offices, early 1920s	31
The three Worcestershire homes of John Corbett	36
Print of Corbett's salt works, about 1875	38
John Corbett's wagon works	41
Various types and packages of salt produced by the Salt Union	41
Brass plaque in St Michael's Church, Stoke Prior	42
John Corbett's Stoke Works School	44
Stoke Works Dispensary Card	47
Mr Corbett's Christmas Beef	47
John and Anna Corbett in their early and later years	51
Postcard of Stoke Works showing the drinking-water fountain	54
Surface mechanism for nos. 1 and 2 brine pits	58
A fine-salt pan	61
Inside a fine-salt panhouse stove	61
The sawmill where squares were sawn into cut lumps	63
Female salt packers wrapping cut lumps, about 1910	63
Broad-salt pans	65
Broad salt being heaped on elm hurdles	65
Loaders at work inside a fine-salt panhouse stove	66
Inside a broad-salt warehouse	66
Two views of the patent machine pans introduced by John Corbett	68
Producing and packing salt cubes in the new mill	69
Farrin's dockyard where formerly Corbett's boats were made and repaired	71
The last salt boat on the Worcester and Birmingham Canal	71
The ICI vacuum plant at Stoke Prior	74
The locomotive *Elephant* and Salt Union wagons	79
Loading Salt Union rail vans	79

Documents and diagrams

Indenture for the creation of the British Alkali Company (BAC) in 1835	15
Agreement for the sale of the Imperial Company to John Corbett, 1867	34
John Corbett's inscription in a Bible presented to Samuel Paxton, 1872	45
Mirrlees-Watson triple-effect brine evaporators	72
Closed- and open-type Krystal 'Oslo' evaporators	73

Maps and plans

Plan of land acquired for the British Rock and Patent Salt Company in 1825	10
Map accompanying the 1834 agreement between Reid and Messrs Burroughs & Cox	10
Plan of Alexander Reid's land and salt works, 1837	17
Birmingham and Gloucester Railway Company's plan of the proposed branch to the BAC's works, 1844	21
Plan of the BAC's works when leased to John Corbett in 1852	28
Plan of the BAC's works when purchased by John Corbett in 1858	30
Plan of the Imperial works leased by F C Hills to John Corbett in 1858	33
Plan of Stoke Prior Salt Works under the Salt Union, early 1920s	59

Stoke Works: notable dates

1812-13 Salt springs discovered in the bed of the canal as it is being dug

1825 William Furnival locates rock salt on the west side of the canal on behalf of the British Rock and Patent Salt Company and begins to mine it

1828 Matthew MacAlister purchases works, finds brine and sinks pits

1831 Works purchased by Alexander Reid and managed by Richard Parker

1836 Imperial Salt and Alkali Co (ISAC) formed

1850 ISAC in the hands of receivers

1851 London auction; no takers. Eventually bought by John Scott for £15,500

1856 F C Hills becomes the owner

1858 Works leased to John Corbett

1828 Jonathan Fardon locates rock salt by boring on the east side of the canal and sinks two shafts; finds brine

1830 Fardon joined by William Gossage to set up chemical and soap works

1835 British Alkali Company (BAC) formed

1836 Gossage chimney erected

1845 John Corbett becomes an agent of BAC

1850 Bankers Rufford and Biggs of Bromsgrove close down, owed £130,000 by BAC

1852 John Corbett obtains lease of the BAC's works

1858 John Corbett purchases BAC works

1867 Ex-Imperial Co bought by Corbett from F C Hills for £25,500. Corbett now sole owner and proprietor of Stoke Works

    1871-2 New works (including machine panhouses) erected on Imperial site

    1889 John Corbett sells his works to the Salt Union for £600,000, and becomes manager of the Worcestershire Division

    1894 John Corbett sells his salt-distribution business and fleet of boats to the Salt Union

    1937 The Salt Union taken over by ICI

    1946-50 Erection of Stoke vacuum plant

    1956 End of open-pan salt production

    1972 Vacuum plant closes down; end of salt production at Stoke Prior

Weights and measures

Throughout the book I have consistently used imperial weights and measures, which were commonly in use throughout the time of the existence of the salt works, without adding the metric equivalent each time. For those, especially younger people, unfamiliar with the imperial system, shillings and pence, and temperatures in Farenheit, the following conversion table may be helpful.

Lengths:
1 inch = 2.5 cm approx.
1 foot (12 inches) = 30 cm approx.
1 yard (3 feet) = 0.91 m approx.

Weights:
1 lb = 454 gm approx.
1 cwt (hundredweight, 112 lb) = 50 kg approx.
1 ton (20 cwt) = 1 tonne approx.

Money:
1d (old penny) = 0.4 p
1s (shilling, 12d) = 5p
£1 = 20 shillings

Temperature: 32°F (Farenheit) = 0.0°C (Celsius)
212°F = 100°C

Introduction and memories of Stoke Works

My interest in the history of Stoke Prior Salt Works arose partly through my researches into the history of the Worcester and Birmingham Canal, astride which the salt works was situated, and partly from the fact that I spent three months in 1986 looking after the United Parish of Stoke Prior, Wychbold and Upton Warren, during which time I met and talked to many old people who had been employed in the works.

In the middle decades of the nineteenth century, as the salt and chemical industries were established and expanded on each side of the canal, a village, consisting mainly of cottages for the employees, began to grow. In the early years the location was known as Stokewich, but soon the village took on the more prosaic name of Stoke Works. Two terraces of houses, Imperial Row and British Row, originally built for key workers alongside the salt works, were later supplemented by the fifty-six dwellings of Sagebury Terrace, six of Shrubbery Terrace and five of Jubilee Terrace along Shaw Lane, built by John Corbett. There were also two rows of old cottages at Causeway Meadows, about half a mile south of the village along and off Shaw Lane, close to what is now the Bowling Green Inn, and in them lived salt workers as well as families who worked on the canal boats. Amenities naturally followed, including shops and public houses.

Articles about Stoke Works village and salt works, written by *Alf Nicklin*, were published at various times in the *Bromsgrove Messenger*. His father and uncles had been employed in the works and he himself worked as a carpenter there under the Salt Union until 1928 when, after training, he became senior production and loading foreman over the open pans. From 1939 to 1960 he lived in the Brine Pump House, some five yards away from the large no. 3 brine well and its engine whose seesaw beam worked the pump twenty-four hours a day. He was also the works safety officer and a qualifed first-aider whose services were often needed in the dangerous environment of the works. An account of Stoke Works village as it was, closely based on the content of talks he gave to various local groups, appears in Appendix C. I am grateful to Mrs Joyce Bastin, Alf's daughter, for permission to use this material.

Another former employee who produced an informative typescript account of salt-making at Stoke Prior is *Len Harris*. Born in 1905, Len left school at the age of thirteen, when his father James Harris, who had been foreman at Droitwich Covercroft Works and had transferred to Stoke in 1906, died. He was apprenticed to the engineer, Alf Rollinson, at Stoke Works and worked as an engineer and fitter there until his retirement. Len has been able to supply firsthand details of the working of the brine pumps and other aspects of salt-making, for which I am grateful. A well-built man, there was an occasion when he got stuck down one of the smaller brine pits and had to be rescued.

Bill Taylor started work as a maintenance painter at Stoke Salt Works on leaving school in January 1938 and, with the exception of five years war service, continued on maintenance work until 1973. Besides having a comprehensive knowledge of the site and buildings of the old and the new plant, he put together an interesting scrapbook, mainly of photographs, from newspapers and the works' magazine. His childhood home, Weston Hall Cottage beside the old Methodist Chapel at the far end of British Row, was at one time the Spotted Leopard pub. His help with memories and illustrations of the works is gratefully acknowledged.

There have been many other men and women whose memories I have tapped when visiting them in their homes. Their reminiscences have contributed to the descriptions in chapter 3 of both the open-pan and the vacuum-plant processes at Stoke. I should like to acknowledge especially the help of the following people:

Ray Lucas, born in 1913, lived at 36 Sagebury Terrace and worked from 1927 to 1934 in no. 24 fine-salt panhouse, helping his father Thomas who was a fine-salt maker. No. 24 was one of five fine-salt panhouses, nos. 22-26, located beside the canal on the west side and nearest to Shaw Lane canal bridge. Between them and the Lymington panhouse was a short canal arm. In Ray's time this canal arm was used to load the last two remaining salt boats, crewed by Jack Wright and Jack Merrell and their partners. Ray married the daughter of William Salcombe, the stationmaster at Stoke Works, and she worked in the new offices of the salt works from 1929 to 1938.

Tom Cocum of Hanbury worked as a young man from 1937 to 1945 as a fine-salt maker on pans of the North Row and Bell Row on the east side of the canal, and for a short time on the patent machine pans on the west side. His father Sam had been for thirty years or more a broad-salt drawer. His wife Hilda worked in the old mill as a salt packer. Like some of his fellow workers, Tom was not sorry to forsake the steamy atmosphere and heavy labour of open-pan salt-making for other employment.

Joe Harrison was a pansmith whose job was to repair the salt pans which, due to corrosion, needed frequent renewal. Born in 1907, he lived when young at 26 Causeway Meadows and went to the village school. He remembered that there were then about one hundred pupils in classes of between fifteen and twenty and that the head teacher was Thomas Williams. His father was a pansmith and at the age of sixteen Joe began, as did all apprentices to the job, as a 'holder-upper' who used long pliers to push up the $\frac{3}{8}$ inch rivets, heated in a coke brazier, from the cramped 2-foot high sooty fire chamber to fasten together the $\frac{3}{8}$ inch thick steel plates of which the salt pans were made. His maternal grandfather James Nicklin, together with his mate 'Baron' Amphlett, had been a night-soil man, whose job was to empty during the night the tin pans from the works' and village privies. They had a hut in the midst of the remains of Corbett's brickworks where they washed out the tin pans. Joe married Maude Lucas who was one of the last salt packers at the old mill. He had three brothers, Bill who drove one of the works' steam locos, *Annie*; another who was a painter; and another who was a sawyer in the old salt mill.

Bill Crowther spent most of his working life at Stoke Works. He started at the age of fourteen in 1927 as a pansmith's rivet-warmer. At the age of twenty-one he became a salt loader for four years and, following that, a fine-salt maker for two years. Then after six years in other employment he returned to the salt works, finishing up as a shunter driver on one of the vacuum plant's two diesel locomotives.

Bob Adams was born in 1889 and was ninety-six years old and with a good memory when I visited him in 1985. His grandfather Thomas Adams had worked for John Corbett and had been presented by his employer with a Bible in 1886. His father Andrew Adams had been a salt maker for eighteen years before working as a secretary in the Salt Union's office and then as a storekeeper. Bob Adams entered the works on leaving school at the age of thirteen in 1902 and retired fifty years later in 1952. He was a skilled carpenter and after six years in the wagon shop, where the Salt Union's vans and wagons were made and repaired, he spent the rest of his time as a pattern maker, making wooden patterns for castings, and as a general carpenter. He remembered sometimes working two hours overtime with other carpenters and bricklayers, loading broad salt into wagons (10-ton loads) on the west side of the canal, using wheelbarrows and shovels, and being paid 4½d per ton. His wife worked for some time as housemaid for Mr W F Hobrough, the engineer to the Worcester and Birmingham Canal, who lived at the Bridge House, Stoke Wharf.

Alfred Robert (Bob) Farmer was born in 1905 in Droitwich and had vivid memories of the salt works there in his younger days and of the sailing barges which took salt along the Droitwich Canal to the River Severn at Hawford. He started work at Stoke in 1920, the year in which the steam engines working the brine pumps were replaced by electric motors. He left in 1952 after thirty-two years service, having been a draughtsman and engineer and, towards the end, foreman of the engineering department. He had a clear and detailed knowledge of the working of the brine pumps and machinery, of the works locomotives, and of the processes involved in the production of the salt.

Mrs Florence Nash, born at 3 Causeway Meadows in 1907, worked as a salt packer in the old mill on the east side of the canal from the age of sixteen until the age of twenty-three when she got married. In those days, as in other occupations such as teaching, women had to give up their jobs at the works when they married. The girl packers were on piecework. For sewing up the two-hundredweight bags of loose salt for export they were paid 3d for every twenty; the rate for wrapping 2-lb blocks was 4d per gross. Mrs Nash kept an interesting scrapbook of photographs of the salt works. Her father James Harper was a pansmith and her brother Victor was an unloader of coal from the wagons. During the First World War, in 1915, Florence travelled down to Sharpness Docks and back on a horse-drawn salt boat with boatman William Blick of 7 Causeway Meadows and his wife Clare, her godmother. The round trip took five or six days and she recalled how Mr Blick lay on his back on the cabin roof to leg the boat through Dunhampstead tunnel.

Edith Healey, born in 1901, worked as a packer in the old mill from 1920 to 1930. Her father William Manning worked in the sawmill producing the cut-lumps for packing. Her grandparents were in charge of the Stoke Prior Reformatory along Shaw Lane and her grandfather founded the Wesleyan Chapel on the works site. Her great-grandfather Mr Harper had worked for John Corbett as he took over the British Alkali Works in 1852, with little pay at first, but as the business prospered he and others were rewarded with lump sums. Edith's mother Elizabeth Harper was a pupil at Stoke Works School when it opened in 1872 and her parents had to pay 1d a week towards her schooling. Edith's brother-in-law Bert Bache was one of many fatalities in the salt works. He was a fine-salt maker, a small man, and he fell over the low pan side into the boiling brine, a not uncommon accident, but inevitably fatal. Another of Edith's memories was of the great freeze-up in the winter of 1915/16, which lasted from six weeks before Christmas to six weeks after, when people could safely walk from one side of the works to the other across the frozen canal.

Jack Merrell spent sixteen years from 1925 as master of a boat which carried salt twice weekly from Stoke Works to the warehouse of Henry Johnson Ltd, Holt Street, Gosta Green, Birmingham. The round trip took three days: on the first day they loaded and reached Tardebigge New Wharf; on the second they arrived in Birmingham, unloaded and returned as far as Gas Street Basin; on the third they arrived back at the Navigation Inn, Stoke Wharf, before closing time at 2.30 pm. Jack's father Dennis and his grandfather Bill Merrell had also worked Johnson's salt boat. Jack's brother Denny, who became a lock-keeper, was his mate at first, then it was Wilfred College for nine years, and finally, at the beginning of World War Two, Tom Mayo. The boat was for many years drawn by a black mule called 'Smoker', kept when not on duty in a paddock by the canal at Whitford Bridge, and described by Jack as 'a real Christian', because he was so cooperative and well-behaved. After a bomb destroyed Johnson's warehouse and their boat in 1941, Jack worked, apart from war service, as a loader at the salt works until his retirement.

Frank Malpas came to Stoke Works from Manchester as the vacuum plant was being set up. Formerly employed as a scaffolder erecting protective wires under high-voltage power lines, he had been blown off and injured in a gale, and found less dangerous work with the ICI, setting up new plants over the country. Once the vacuum plant was in operation at Stoke Works he was retained as one of four foremen who supervised the continuous working of the plant operated by three shifts of workmen. He retired in 1970 after more than twenty years service. His considerable experience and knowledge of the working of the vacuum plant has been an invaluable source of information. One of his earliest memories was of Walter Stanley who sounded the 'Bull', the steam-operated works siren on top of the old boiler house, with an eye on his watch, until it was done away with in 1950.

Arthur Harris began work at Stoke in 1927 and finished forty-five years later when the works closed in 1972. He married Phyllis Wright, niece of salt boatman Jack Wright, whom he met when they both worked in the new mill where salt cubes were cut and packed. After service in World War Two Arthur returned to work for four or five years as a broad-salt drawer in the 'new broads', the two broad-salt panhouses near the main works entrance off the Hanbury Road. When the vacuum plant opened in 1950 he transferred to it and was a filterman throughout the twenty-two years of its operation. With Frank Malpas and others he took part in the annual clean-out of the plant's large boiler which took place during the August holiday when salt production was temporarily halted.

Ron Usher was employed as a loader and deputy driver of the works diesel locomotives, and at times deputy foreman, from 1949 to 1971. I am grateful to him for the loan of his copy of the large-scale print of Corbett's salt works and of old photographs of the works taken from the large brine reservoir. His knowledge of the geography of the works has been most helpful.

Charles Creese worked as a fitter on the vacuum plant from 1949 to 1972 and therefore has a first-hand knowledge of the component parts, layout and machinery of the plant. He was also works representative and attended meetings of the local works council and the ICI Board.

Besides the information about Stoke Works derived from these and other former employees, I have to acknowledge the assistance given by others less directly involved. These include *Miss Marjorie Honeybourne* who for many years was the postmistress in John B Wilson's shop in the village. Her father William Honeybourne worked in the offices of the salt works. Her grandfather William Harris, of 10 Sagebury Terrace, was a broad-salt drawer and earned 12 shillings a week in the early 1900s. Another grandfather George Honeybourne, who retired in 1934 after sixty years service, was a wagon weigher at the works, and his records of the tare weight of wagons and vans for 1892-4 have survived. He also kept a diary of local events, including such entries as '1894 Good Friday — Bull Blowed at 5 O'clock'; 'First Spring Buffer Truck out March 22/94'; 'John Barker Killed on line by 442 Van March 28/99'; 'No beer to be brought on these Works by Order W.J. Jny.1/04'; 'Will Honeybourne run into Canal with his Bike July 14 1904'; '*Elephant* in Shop for repairs July 1909'; '1911 Hottest Summer for years since 1868'; and 'Motor Buses started to run to Bromsgrove October 1913'.

Mrs Sue Abel has an interesting collection of photographs and souvenirs of Stoke Salt Works and the village. Her father Joe Bloomfield was a carpenter in the works. Her grandfather Edward Bloomfield looked after the stables and the horses which were used to pull railway wagons and vans about the works. He and his wife Agnes and their ten children lived in GWR House between the railway bridges in Shaw Lane and, in return for a peppercorn rent, they looked after the stationmaster's fire and lamps on the nearby station.

Information about the earlier history of Stoke Works has been derived from a number of sources including documents in Worcester Record Office, newspapers, parish records, census records from 1841 to 1891, and canal committee minutes. I am grateful to the late Mr Michael Young of Bromsgrove, postal historian, for letting me have copies of letters relating to the British Alkali Company and to John Corbett; and to Mr John Homer Fardon for information about his family history and especially about Jonathan Fardon who set up the first salt works on the east side of the canal.

For a comprehensive account of the life and achievements of John Corbett *John Corbett Pillar of Salt 1817-1901* by Barbara Middlemass and Joe Hunt (Saltway Press, 2nd edition 1995) provides a wealth of information based on extensive research and some imagination. Curiously, the authors seem not to have known that Corbett's first home for some six years following his marriage was Rigby Hall, Finstall, and not Stoke Grange which only later became the family home following the move from Rigby Hall in 1862. However, the book does provide a fascinating insight into the character of John Corbett, into his unsettled family life and the eventual breakup of his marriage, and into his social, political and benevolent activities, the details of which are outside the scope of this present book.

My greatest debt of gratitude for a wealth of technical and background information, much of it in the form of photocopies of articles about the history of the salt and allied chemical industries, is owed to George Twigg of Sandbach, Cheshire. Himself an enthusiasic historian of these industries, he has generously shared his knowledge and has sought out information where necessary from the Salt Museum at Northwich and other local sources, and from various individuals. His advice and help have been much appreciated, and especially much technical information about salt production by the vacuum process. One of his informants has been John Whalley, now living in Cheshire, who was foreman fitter at Stoke Prior vacuum plant from 1964 to 1972 and who had earlier been involved with the commissioning of the plant in 1950.

In addition to these and other people, I am also grateful for the help of staff at Worcester Record Office, both at County Hall and at St Helen's, and to those at Bromsgrove Public Library and the Droitwich Heritage Centre.

Most of the photographs of the salt works are from the Stoke Works copy of the Salt Union Album of 1923 which is now kept in the Meadow Bank rock-salt mine offices at Winsford. From it prints were kindly supplied by George Twigg. For photographs of John and Anna Corbett I am grateful to the Droitwich Heritage Centre and to Mrs Anna Denlegh-Maxwell, a great-granddaughter of John Corbett. Others are from various individuals including Len Harris, Bob Dutton, Ron Usher, Sue Abel and Jack Merrell, to whom I am also grateful. The photographs of the homes of John Corbett, the plaque in Stoke Prior Church, and the vacuum plant are my own. I also gratefully acknowledge permission to reproduce copies of documents and plans from Worcester Record Office; and from Donald Ashmore the inscription inside the Bible in his possession, given by John Corbett to Samuel Paxton.

Alan White, February 1996

Chapter 1

The Pre-Corbett Era: 1825-52

Beginnings on the west side of the canal

It was the year 1825 that saw the beginnings of a salt industry beside the Worcester and Birmingham Canal in the parish of Stoke Prior. In early legal documents relating to the salt works the location is called Stokewich, and this would have been a pleasanter and more appropriate name for the industrial village which came into being there than Stoke Works, by which both the village and the industrial site became known. At neighbouring Droitwich, three miles to the south-west, salt had been obtained from underground springs since the time of the Roman occupation. The strata of rock salt under Droitwich extended to the north-west and contained a number of subterranean brine streams, but it was not until the Worcester and Birmingham Canal was being cut through the parish of Stoke Prior in 1812 and 1813 that the presence of salt in that location was realised. There is a reference in a minute book of the committee of the canal company to salt springs found in the bed of the canal as it was being dug. Little did the local inhabitants of this rural area realise, as their peace was disturbed by the creation of the canal, that because of the discovery of salt deposits, there would be, within a few years, the establishment of industrial buildings, pits and chimneys, the creation of an industrial village and a new means of employment for many local people.

Until 1823 there was a government tax on salt of £30 per ton, which discouraged the production and the purchase of salt. In 1823 the tax was reduced to £6 per ton, and then in 1825 it was completely abolished. The price of English salt thus fell from around £31 per ton before 1823 to around £1 per ton from 1825. There was now an incentive for salt to be found and marketed, and it was around 1825 that the possibility of finding a salt seam below ground, near Shaw Lane Bridge over the canal at Stoke Prior, began to be investigated. Dr Charles Hastings, in his paper *The Salt Springs of Worcestershire* published in 1835, tells us that 'a brine-smeller was ... sent for from Cheshire, and after examining the Country, he pronounced that there was salt to be found at Stoke Prior'. This brine-smeller, Hastings went on to explain, 'attached great importance to what he called brine-slips, that is a slipping or subsidence of the red marl in which strata of salt were often found'. We are not told by Hastings the name of the brine-smeller nor who it was who sent for him, but he was almost certainly summoned by William Furnival whose involvement, as that of Jonathan Fardon a few years later, was linked with developments in the salt industry in nearby Droitwich.

Furnival was a restless eccentric character, believed to have been a Liverpool salt merchant, who became obsessed with the idea that the traditional, rather inefficient, furnace-heated open-pan method of salt production could be improved upon, and salt produced more cheaply, by the use of steam-heating. Early in 1822 he travelled widely, observing steam-heating plant already being used in chemical processes. He obtained the manufacturing rights of a patent (no. 4805 granted 19 June 1823) in the name of James Smith of Port Seton, near Prestonpans on the Firth of Forth in Scotland, for an apparatus designed to apply steam to the boiling and concentration of solutions. In October 1822, with the financial help of a relative John Furnival, he obtained the lease of some property in Droitwich, and during 1823 set up a salt works to use a steam-heating process. In this, a flat-topped oblong boiler, besides heating a salt pan on top of it, also supplied piped steam to heat a number of other salt pans. In September 1824 Furnival sold out to Thomas Fowler, Jonathan Fardon, William Lloyd and Thomas Langley and went and leased some land at Anderton in Cheshire for another salt works based on the same principles. For various practical reasons it seems that these early attempts to use steam were not very successful, but Furnival was granted his own patent (no. 5046 on 4 December 1824) at the same time as a similar one was obtained by William Weston Young of Droitwich.

The spring of 1825 saw a craze for the creation of joint stock companies, and Furnival was a leading light in the establishment of the British Rock and Patent Salt Company with headquarters in London and a proposed share capital of £2.5 million. It was intended that Furnival's and Young's steam-heating patents should be used in brine works acquired by the company. Furnival became a director, having sold his interests to the company, and during the summer of 1825 he was busy exploring for brine in various places including Stoke Prior. He it was who, with the help of the experienced 'brine-smeller' from Cheshire, found rock salt on the west side of the canal. A six-acre site between the west side of the canal and Shaw Lane, together with a one-acre site beween the east side of the canal and the road to Hanbury, were soon purchased for £408 8s 6d and were in the joint ownership of Furnival, William Weston Young and Alexander Law, directors of the new company.

It was reported in *Berrow's Worcester Journal* on 13 October 1825 that the 'British Rock and Patent Salt Company are erecting works at Stoke Prior'. A few years later, in May 1833, Furnival, languishing in a debtors' prison, produced a 'Statement of Fact' in which he presented his case to Parliament, and in it he claimed to have searched for rock salt and brine in the Droitwich area and to have located these beside the canal at Stoke Prior. Furnival's involvement at Stoke Prior soon came to an end for, as his company suffered with others in the financial panic of the autumn of 1825 and had to reduce its intended share capital to £500,000, he left it and went off to France to pursue his interests there. In 1826 Alexander Law paid £500 to Furnival and Young to become the sole owner of the land and works already in hand. In 1827 these were mortgaged for £3,000 to Joseph Young and William Weston Young, trading as Joseph Young and Son. In the same year Alexander Law died and the land and premises were put up for sale by public auction at the Star Inn in Worcester on 3 August 1828. The purchaser was Matthew MacAlister, who paid £1,580 for the site and the works which were still of very limited extent and, so far, only mining rock salt.

Jonathan Fardon's works on the east side of the canal

Jonathan Fardon and Thomas Langley, who had taken over the management of the former Droitwich Salt Works of William Furnival in 1824, were soon involved in the establishment of a new company, the Droitwich Patent Salt Company, which came into being on 4 May 1825, with a proposed share capital of £125,000 in units of £25. This new company agreed to buy Fardon and Langley's works for £70,000 by instalments of cash and shares, the two men becoming managers of the company, and it also bought up all but one of the other salt works in Droitwich. However, the promise of greatly increased production using steam-heated pans failed to be achieved and it was the remaining directly-fired open pans which maintained supplies. The committee of the company became dissatisfied with progress and there was also some dispute over financial and legal matters which led to Fardon and Langley being dismissed from the management in July 1827, and they finally severed their connections with the Droitwich Patent Salt Company in February 1828, their interests and the management passing to Messrs Clay and Newman.

Jonathan Fardon and his associates in Droitwich must have followed with interest the developments at Stoke Prior, following the setting up of works to mine rock salt there in 1825. Fardon himself was an enterprising man, ready, as we have seen, to try out new methods of salt production, and he had been experimenting at Droitwich with the manufacture of synthetic barilla or soda ash from salt. Forced to give up his Droitwich interests, he now turned to Stoke Prior in the hope of finding and exploiting rock salt and brine on the east side of the canal. Early in 1828 he hired labour and machinery and succeeded in locating beds of rock salt some 300 feet down below the red marl. He began to negotiate for the land and on 1 April 1829 he acquired the copyhold of the site called the Lower Leasowes, just over eight acres in extent alongside the canal, upon which, it was stated, he had already established a 'Chemical Manufactory'. The following report appeared in *Berrow's Worcester Journal* on 10 June 1830:

> Mr. Jonathan Fardon purchased some land at Stoke Prior nearly two years ago, and the presence of rock salt was ascertained a few weeks after by boring. It was, however, fully expected that the brine lay above the rock, and that the latter could not be obtained. The fresh water springs at this place are so very numerous, so very powerful, and lie so deep in the earth, that in order to obtain the brine it was necessary to sink a pair of pits, and, to accomplish this, a powerful steam engine was requisite; this being erected, a water shaft was first sunk to the depth of nearly 120 feet, and, subsequently, another shaft, which it was expected would

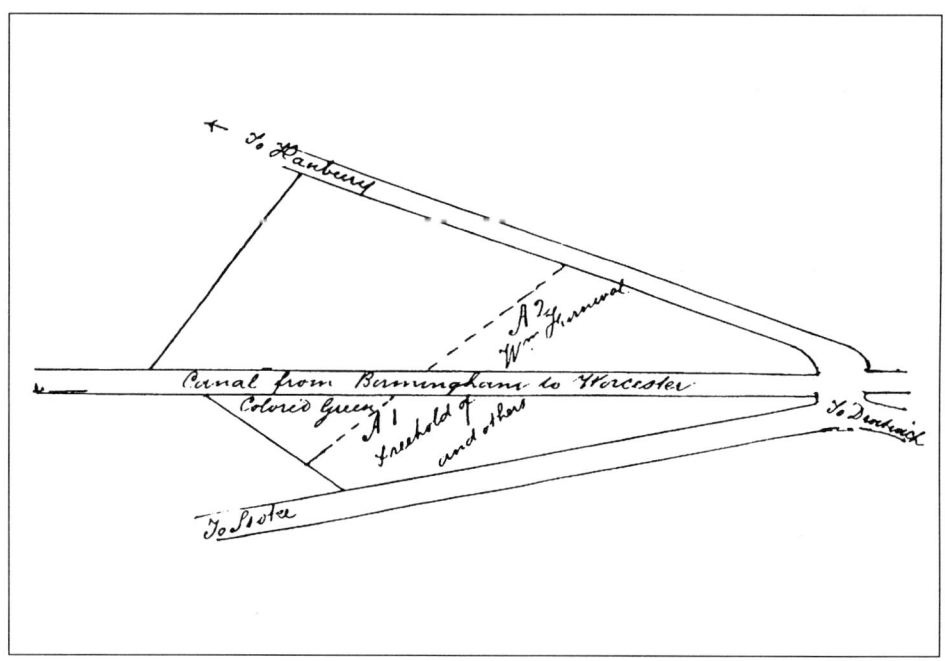

Plan of the freehold and leasehold land at Stoke Prior acquired by Furnival, Young and Law, on behalf of the British Rock and Patent Salt Company, in 1825.

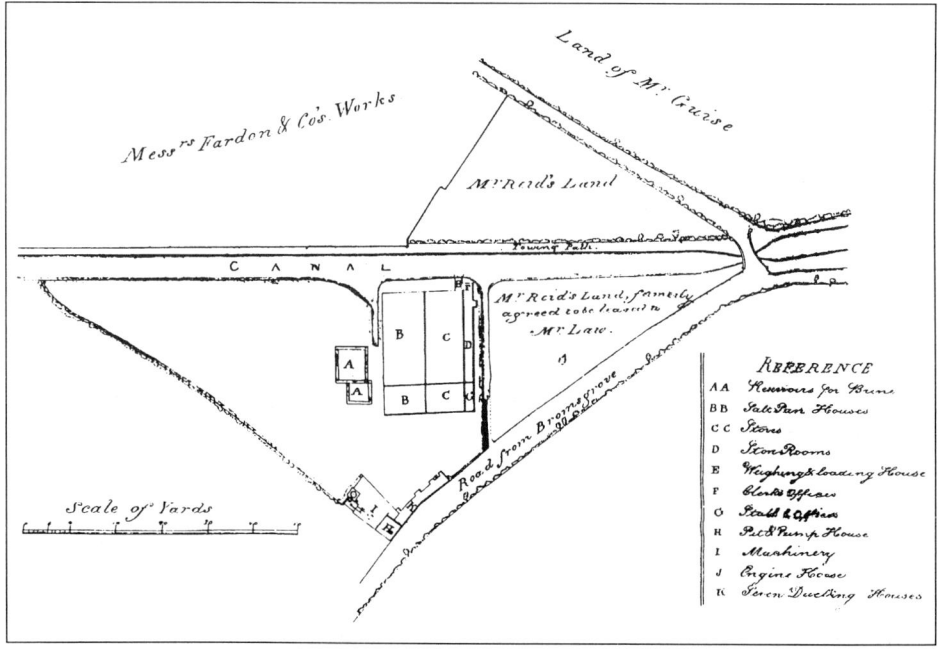

Map accompanying the agreement of September 1834 whereby Alexander Reid leased his salt works to Messrs Burroughs & Cox for 21 years at an annual rent of £800.

have proved a brine shaft. In order to make this latter shaft perfectly free from fresh water, it was necessary to case it entirely with iron for nearly 150 feet from the surface; this being done and the first attempt to keep out the springs having succeeded, it was expected that by boring again from the bottom of this shaft a good spring of brine would have been found, but, as before, rock only was discovered. It was therefore determined on sinking the shaft to it; at this sinking the workmen have now been at work night and day for about seven months, and have, within the last four or five weeks, passed through several thin strata of rock salt. They are now in a stratum (at the depth of nearly 400 feet) the thickness of which is not yet ascertained, but which, it is not doubted, will prove abundant, and ultimately repay the enormous outlay. The ground passed through, below the iron casing, was very similar to the upper strata, only of so compact a nature, that steel chisels would not stand against it, and nearly the whole of the sinking has been effected by the force of gunpowder. It is not a little singular, that during the last five years, from 8 to 10,000l. have been expended within 100 yards of this spot in endeavouring to get a shaft free from fresh water; the workmen have now only sunk a depth of about fifty yards. At about this depth a copious supply of hydrogen gas has come into the pit, and several explosions have been the consequence. So much for the uncertainty and danger attending mining operations. Not withstanding the compactness of the ground below the iron casing, such is the peculiar nature of it, that it was necessary quickly to follow the workmen with casing the whole depth of the shaft, to prevent the sides falling in on them. Only a few days' exposure to the air produced this extraordinary change.

This slightly confusing newspaper report does confirm that from 1825 attempts had been made by boring and sinking shafts to find brine and rock salt, and that the many springs of fresh water in the surface layers of the ground and the depth of the strata of rock salt below the surface had made the operations very difficult. However, in 1828 Fardon had been successful. In a letter to the canal company dated 24 September 1828 he stated that he was about to put up some works on the banks of the canal at Stoke Prior and wanted to know the lowest rate of tonnage on bricks from Hanbury Wharf to Stoke, also the tonnage on lime from Dunhampstead to Stoke and on coal to Stoke. In reply Fardon was informed that the tonnages would be 3d per ton per mile on bricks, 10d per ton on lime from Dunhampstead, and 3 shillings per ton on coal along the canal to Stoke. By June 1830 Fardon's works were in an advanced state, for that month he applied to the canal company for permission to build a wharf wall, two boats in length, fronting his chemical works, and to make openings between his sluices (canal arms) and the canal and to erect towing path bridges over the sluices being made. The canal was already being used by Danks and Company to carry bricks for the construction of the works.

At the end of 1830 Fardon was joined by William Gossage, an enterprising and innovative chemist, to develop and manage the chemical side, and the business became Fardon, Gossage and Company. Gossage (1799-1877) was a native of Lincolnshire, the youngest of a family of thirteen children, who had become interested in chemistry through being apprenticed at the age of twelve to his uncle, a chemist and druggist in Chesterfield. He experimented and studied chemical theory and processes in books and papers and, following his apprenticeship, he moved to Leamington and set up his own business as a druggist. He developed an interest in industrial chemistry and, following his arrival at Stoke Prior, constructed the chemical works in which the already well-established Leblanc process was to be used (as later described) in the manufacture of soda and other alkaline substances. Gossage's association with the Stoke Works was to last twenty years. During this time he lived with his wife and sons Alfred and Frederick at Rashwood, between Stoke Prior and Droitwich. With the chemical works well established, he was involved in the 1840s with research into paint pigments in Birmingham and into copper and zinc smelting in South Wales. In 1850 he left Stoke Works for Widnes, Cheshire, taking with him some of his employees. In Widnes he set up a chemical works for the manufacture of alkali and soap. and during the latter part of the nineteenth century the soap produced by William Gossage & Sons was well known and widely used at home and abroad.

Progress on the west side of the canal

At the same time as Fardon and Gossage's salt and chemical works were being developed on the east side of the canal, Matthew MacAlister was busy developing his works on the west side and, having located a spring of brine, had sunk two pits. The following report appeared in *Berrow's Worcester Journal*, 26 August 1830:

> We understand that the pits recently sunk by Mr. M'Allister, on the opposite side of the Worcester Canal to the mine of rock salt lately found at Stoke Prior, are now complete. On tapping the brine a few days ago, at the depth of 97 yards, the spring was so strong that it rose upwards of 40 yards in two hours; since which it has increased to 74 yards, or within 23 yards of the top of the pit. Steam engines have been erected upon both works, and every preparation is being made for commencing operations within the present month.

During the previous month the committee of works of the canal company had agreed to allow MacAlister to get stone at his own expense from its Dusthouse quarry at Tardebigge to provide coping stones for the sluice at his works at Stoke Prior, and he was allowed free tonnage on the conveyance of this stone. In 1831 the canal company received the following information in a letter dated 21 March from John Bradley, agent:

> The Salt Works lately belonging to Mr. Macalister were last month purchased by Mr. Reed of the firm of Alexr. Reed & Co., Carriers, Liverpool and one of the Proprietors of the extensive Anderton Salt Works, Cheshire. All Tonnages owing by Mr. Macalister, as well as all future Amounts, you will please charge to Mr. Reed.

The canal committee agreed that Mr Reid should be allowed the usual quarterly credit. Alexander Reid paid £4,896 to MacAlister for the freehold of part of the land, the copyhold of the rest, and for the works established upon it. To manage his newly acquired works, Reid soon appointed Richard Parker of Hambro' Wharf in the city of London. Parker was to play a major role in the development and management of the salt and chemical works during the next twenty years or so.

In 1834 part of Reid's salt works was leased to Messrs William Burrows and Richard Cox at a rent of £800 per annum. A map accompanying the lease agreement shows the works at that time were on a small scale compared to those of Fardon and Gossage. They consisted only of a single building between two canal arms containing fine- and broad- salt pans and drying stoves, store rooms and offices, as well as a weighing and loading house beside the canal, two small brine reservoirs and, at the north-west corner of the site, close to the road from Bromsgrove (Shaw Lane), one brine pit with pump house, engine house and machinery, and a terrace of seven dwelling houses (later to be called Imperial Row).

In 1835 an agreement was signed by Reid and Parker for Parker to purchase from Reid for £12,000 the freehold and copyhold land and the works on the west side of the canal, and also a small area of Reid's one-acre site on the east side at £1 per square yard for a new brine pit, the work to be financed by Reid. Messrs Burrows and Cox were to have the use of the new pit on Mondays, Wednesdays and Fridays, Reid having the option on the remaining weekdays to supply any new works he might build, each party to be responsible for the cost of working the pumping engine on their allotted days. A similar sharing arrangement was agreed for the use of the old pit on the west side. The new pit and its engine house were under construction in 1836. At the same time a metal footbridge was constructed over the canal opposite the new pit and it carried a pipe through which the brine was pumped to a raised brine reservoir tank on the west side of the canal.

Each of the salt works entered into negotiations with the canal company over drawbacks (or reductions) on tonnages. In 1831 the canal company, anticipating an upsurge in salt traffic, agreed to a drawback of 1s 6d from the statutuary 3s 6d per ton on salt carried along the canal from Stoke Prior. Also at the end of 1831 Fardon, Gossage & Co were allowed free passage along the canal of soapers' ashes for the three months of December, January and February, and thereafter a drawback of 1s 6d from 3s 6d, as for salt.

Fardon and Gossage's works

In his 1835 pamphlet *The Salt Springs of Worcestershire* Dr Charles Hastings, who had visited the works at Stoke Prior, gives an interesting account of developments there. His report concentrated on the works of Fardon and Gossage which were then at a far more advanced stage than those of their rivals across the canal, where several changes of ownership had delayed development. We are told that at first Messrs Fardon and Gossage had mined the rock salt, but this was an expensive operation, so they introduced a supply of fresh water to dissolve it and so converted the mine into an artificial brine spring and pumped up the brine. Very soon, however, no more water was needed as a 'communication' took place between a natural brine spring and the mine. The brine thus obtained had a specific gravity of 1.207, being fully saturated with salt, whereas that furnished by the spring at the works of Mr A Reid on the other side of the canal had a specific gravity of only 1.150. By 1835 the two works at Stoke Prior were producing between them about 15,000 tons of salt per annum, about half the total amount of salt then being produced at Droitwich, and over two hundred people were employed in the Stoke Prior Works producing salt and chemicals.

Dr Hastings described how the various types of salt were produced by evaporation of the brine, as follows:

> In procuring the salt from the brine, the temperature required for boiling the solution is equal to 229 degrees of Farenheit thermometer. This process yields what is usually called fine salt, the same that is employed for domestic purposes. Another kind, called broad salt, is made by evaporation at a lower temperature, by which the crystals being formed more slowly, and in a fluid not agitated by boiling, become more perfect in their form and of a greater size. This kind of salt is chiefly exported, and employed for curing provisions. When the process of evaporation is conducted still more slowly, very large crystals are obtained, which are sold under the name of British Bay Salt. During the making of fine salt, a considerable proportion of the salt attaches itself to the pan, and by the influence of the heat it becomes hard and adheres very closely to the iron plates. This accumulates to such a thickness as to render it necessary to be removed once a week, which is effected by allowing the fires to burn out, and then beating the cake with large hammers. The scale thus breaks up into pieces, varying in size from a foot square and two inches thick, to smaller dimensions. This product is called pan scale or picking, and when broken down to a coarse powder is found to be exceedingly useful as a dressing for light sandy soil. The large masses of pan scale are particularly suited to be laid down in grazing fields for the use of cattle, and its employment is strongly recommended to graziers, as the most benficial results have been obtained from its use.
>
> The pans employed on these operations are made of wrought iron plates, joined together by rivetting, and they vary considerably in dimensions. Those now in use for making fine salt are usually about 20 feet long by 20 feet wide and one foot deep. A pan of this size yields about 20 tons of salt per week. The pan is fixed in a building suitably arranged for the escape of vapour, and immediately contiguous to this are situated the drying stoves. The fire employed for evaporation is so placed that the smoke flues are passed through the drying stoves before arriving at the chimney, and in this way sufficient heat is obtained for the drying process. As the evaporation goes on slowly in making broad salt, more extensive vessels are required to yield a sufficient quantity; some of them are upwards of 100 feet long. These pans at Droitwich are heated by fires, but at Stoke Prior the heat is applied through the medium of steam. The brine in this process is generally kept at a temperature between 160 and 170 degrees. The broad salt does not require to be dried in a stove; it is therefore thrown loose into a warehouse ready for exportation.
>
> The labour of making salt is usually paid for by contract, at the rate of two shillings or two shillings and sixpence per ton weight. A considerable part of this labour is performed by females, who are said to withstand better the influence of heat in the drying stoves, where much exertion is used in moving the blocks of salt into various situations to promote and complete their perfect drying. The temperature of the stoves ranges from 120 to 130 degrees. The remuneration

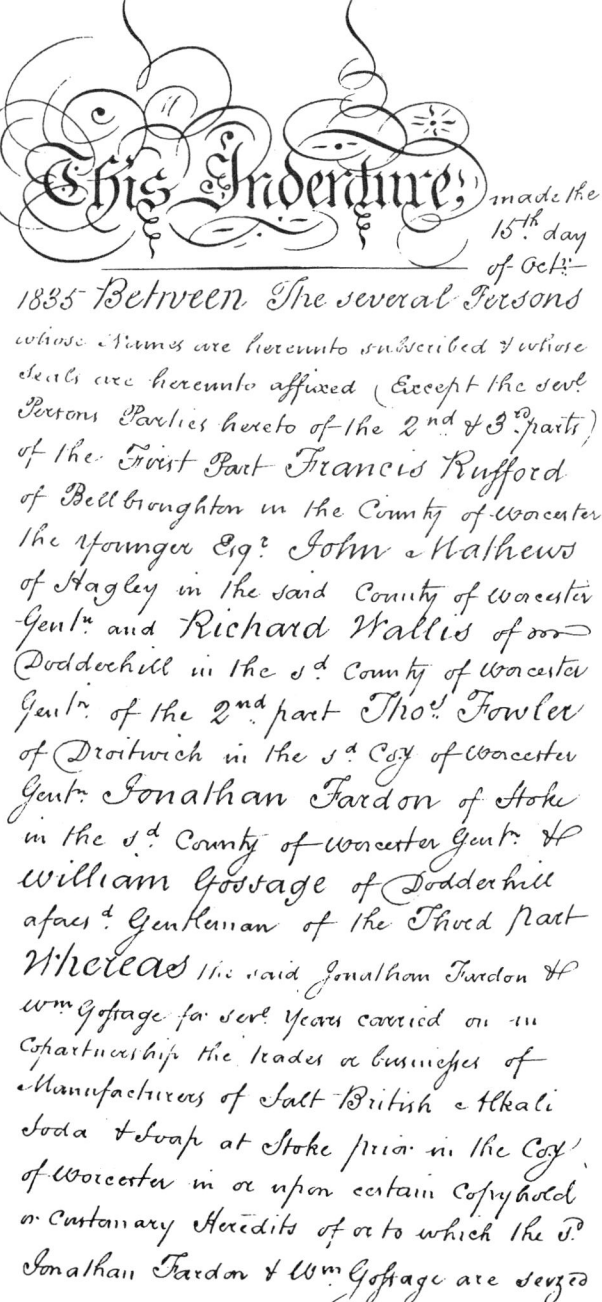

The first page of the deed of settlement under which the British Alkali Company was formed in 1835.

obtained by the work-people varies from fifteen to twenty-five shillings per week, according to the situation they occupy, either as contractors for the working of a pan, or labourers employed under the contractors.

Besides the manufacture of salt, Messrs Fardon and Gossage were by 1835 also making use of it in the production of washing soda and medicinal sodium carbonate, caustic soda (sodium hydroxide) used in the manufacture of soap at the works, and chloride of lime (bleaching powder). The chemical processes involved are decribed by Hastings:

> The first decomposition of salt is effected by treating it with sulphuric acid, which is prepared at the manufactory in immense leaden chambers. The combustion of sulphur by atmospheric air is conducted in vessels connected with these chambers, and the vapour produced being mixed with nitrous gas and water becomes converted into liquid sulphuric acid. By decomposition with the sulphuric acid the salt is converted into sulphate of soda, which is then mixed with the requisite proportions of lime and ground coal and then submitted to igneous fusion in furnaces of brickwork. The product from this operation consists chiefly of carbonate of soda, but mixed with sulphur and lime. It is dissolved in water, and by subsequent processes is rendered nearly pure, and at length obtained in beautiful crystals. In this state the soda is adapted to the use of manufacturers and to common domestic purposes. A portion is submitted to a further purification, and being combined with an additional quantity of carbonic acid, it furnishes medicinal carbonate of soda. A portion of the solution obtained from the rough soda is treated with lime to abstract the carbonic acid, and is then obtained in the state of caustic soda, suitable for the manufacture of soap, of which a large quantity is prepared at these works.

Dr Hastings went on to describe briefly how chloride of lime was manufactured using some of the hydrochloric acid produced by the initial reaction of sulphuric acid upon salt. He did not describe the soap-making process. In this, oil and fats, such as palm oil and tallow, were usually boiled together with caustic soda. This produced a paste and then when salt was added soap curds were formed, leaving behind an aqueous liquor. The curds were worked into the finished soap and the liquor was treated to extract glycerine and recover the salt for reuse.

The British Alkali Company

The Fardon and Gossage Salt and Chemical Works were evidently prospering and ready to expand, and in a footnote Hastings mentions that 'the Proprietors have formed a public company, called the British Alkali Company' and praises the proprietors of the Worcester and Birmingham Canal Company for encouraging the new company by reducing their tonnages to the mutual benefit of both enterprises.

The British Alkali Company (BAC) was constituted by a deed of settlement (a debenture or legal agreement) dated 15 October 1835. Fardon and Gossage sold the works to the new company for £120,000. The initial capital of the BAC

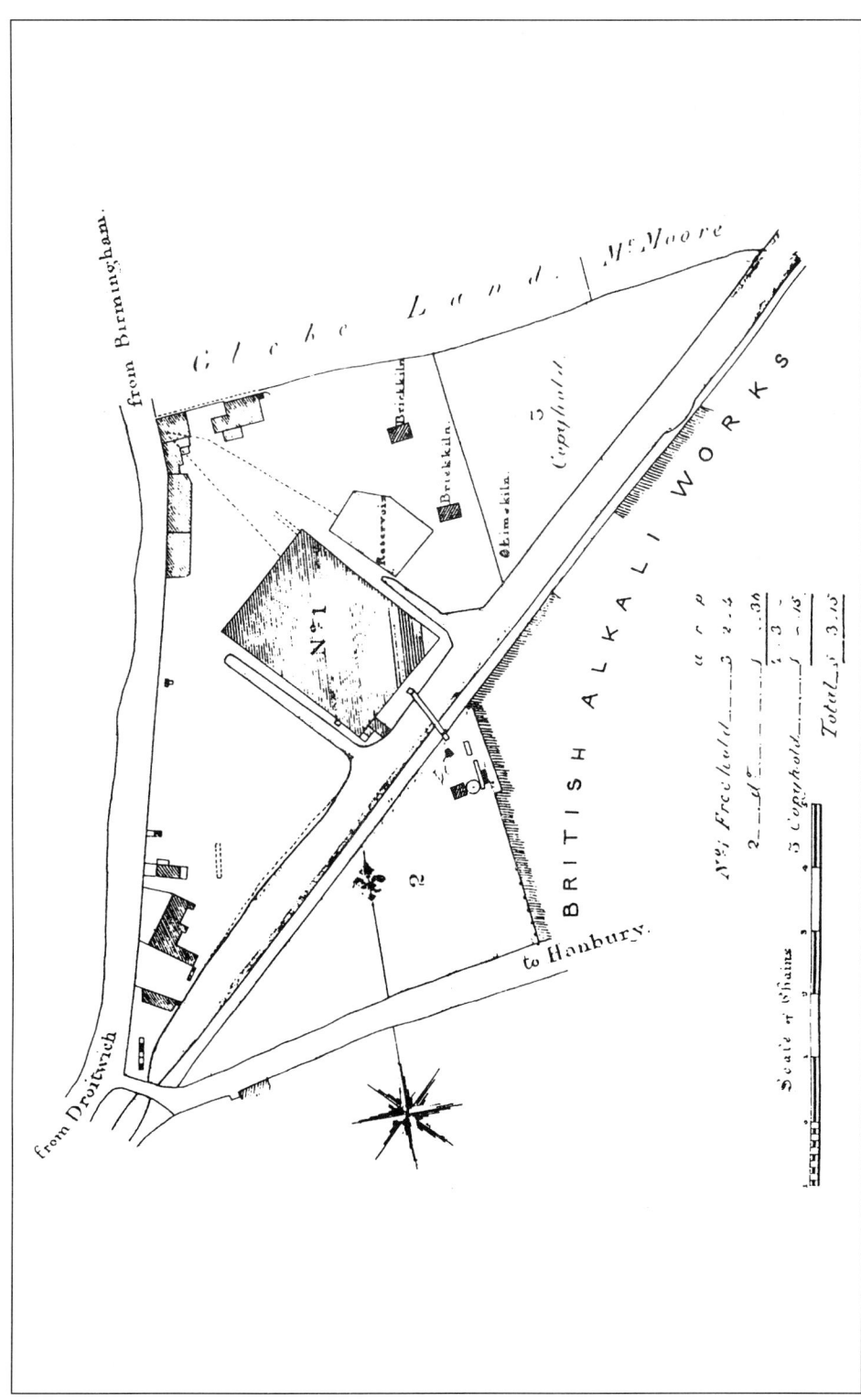

1837 plan of Alaxander Reid's land and salt works as taken over by the Imperial Salt and Alkali Company. Dotted lines show the course of brine pipes from the old pit. Also shown are the new pit and engine pump house and the new footbridge carrying the brine pipe over the canal.

was £150,000 divided into 6,000 shares of £25 each, with an option (soon exercised) to raise £50,000 more. The following year an Act of Parliament was passed (Royal Assent, 19 May 1836) to 'enable the British Alkali Company to sue and be sued in the Name of the Secretary, or any one Member, for the time being, of the said Company'. This gave the BAC a legal identity, enabling contracts to be entered into, property owned, and debts incurred by the company as a corporate body and not, as was otherwise the case, by individual shareholders.

The original directors of the company were Jonathan Fardon, his brother-in-law Thomas Fowler, William Gossage, John Matthews, Richard Wallis, and Francis Rufford. Of these, Rufford, Fardon and Gossage were active in managing the new company. Francis Rufford was the power behind the Bromsgrove bank Rufford, Biggs and Co which had helped to finance the setting up of the salt and chemical works, and which was owed some £50,000 when the BAC was formed and bought out Fardon and Gossage for £120,000. Earlier, in 1832, under financial pressure, the copyhold of the land and premises of the works had been surrendered to Francis Rufford and his father Philip, who were then partners in the Bromsgrove bank in which Fardon, Gossage and Co held their accounts. Rufford became chairman of the new company and controller of its finances; he managed the business side, having a hand in the buying of raw materials, such as tallow and palm oil used in soap-making, and the marketing of the firm's products. Fardon continued to manage the production of salt and Gossage the chemical works.

One of the first decisions of the BAC was to allow Gossage to erect beside his chemical works a tall and massive chimney 309 feet high, 26 feet in diameter at the base, 9 feet across at the top and with brickwork 2 feet thick. It had a substantial limestone base, required about half-a-million bricks, and took nine months to erect. The purpose of this structure was not just to dissipate into the upper atmosphere the harmful hydrochloric acid fumes given off by the action of sulphuric acid upon salt to produce sodium sulphate in the Leblanc process, but to house apparatus invented by Gossage to absorb as much as possible of the hydrochloric acid gas to produce a concentrated solution. He had conducted experiments in a disused windmill near the works, passing the acid gas through a deep bed of small lumps of coke through which a spray of water percolated downwards. The extensive moistened surface absorbed the gas, and as the water descended it became saturated. By this means most of the acid fumes which had previously damaged crops and vegetation and endangered human health in the vicinity were eliminated. The Gossage chimney had within it a smaller chimney, about a quarter of its height, and this was evidently the 'acid absorption tower', as such similar structures using Gossage's process came to be called. The big chimney was commissioned ceremonially on 6 November 1836 by Mrs Gossage. A few weeks later, on 24 December 1836, Gossage was granted the patent (BP 7267/36) for his invention. With the later demise of the chemical works in the Corbett era, the chimney became the smoke stack of his new engine house and on it was mounted the 'bull', or buzzer, which summoned employees to their shifts and provided time signals to the population for miles around. Eventually in 1924

Aerial photograph of Stoke Works taken around 1920.

Aerial photograph taken after 1924 when the big chimney was truncated.

the top 57 feet of the chimney were removed for safety reasons, but the truncated structure, 252 feet high, remained in use for many more years until it was finally demolished following the ending of the open-pan method of salt production in 1956.

Another early decision of the BAC was to lease from the Gloucester and Berkeley Canal Co a canal wharf and warehouse at Gloucester adjacent to Hempstead canal bridge. The lease, agreed in March 1836, was for sixty three years at an annual rent of £34 6s. The 300-feet long warehouse fronted a canal lay-by where boats could tie up and discharge their cargo of salt at this distribution centre.

The Imperial Salt and Alkali Company

On the west side of the canal, the Imperial Salt and Alkali Company (ISAC) was established in 1836 to acquire the works of Messrs Reid and Parker and to provide funds for the settlement of debts and the expansion of operations including the production of chemicals and the making of soap. For his part in the business Richard Parker was to be paid £20,000 and allotted 2,000 shares in the company. The company was authorised to raise capital of £75,000 in 6,000 shares of £12 10s., and empowered to borrow up to £50,000 more. Its six directors were Messrs Robert and James Morrell of Oxford, who were also the company's bankers, H Morrell of London, J Hansford of Oxford, J Parker of Bicester and R Garrett of London. For a time the works were managed by Richard Parker and produced salt, vitriol (sulphuric acid) and soda. The chemical works were erected from the designs and under the supervision of Professor Clark of Aberdeen. The building of a wharf wall in 1836 was superintended by the canal company's engineer, George Rew, and in 1837 Richard Parker negotiated with the canal company a tonnage rate of 1 shilling a ton only on bricks conveyed by canal from Hanbury Wharf for extensions to the works.

Arrival of the Birmingham and Gloucester Railway

During the early years, transport of coal, lime, mundic (iron sulphide used in making sulphuric acid), bricks and other materials to the works, and of salt and chemicals from the works, was almost entirely by canal boat, and the parish registers and census returns for Stoke Prior show a number of local men employed as boatmen. In 1840 the Birmingham and Gloucester Railway was constructed through Stoke Prior parish, to pass close to the ISAC. It opened through to Birmingham in 1841, and soon the ISAC works were served by a siding. But the BAC works were cut off from the railway by the canal; so in 1844 the Birmingham and Gloucester Railway Company produced a plan and sections of a proposed branch to cross the canal by a bridge into the works. The canal company, anxious to stave off railway competition, opposed in September 1844 an application from the BAC for the construction of this bridge. However, in August 1845 an Act of Parliament was passed which included the

authorisation of a short branch from the main line into the works, to be constructed within twelve months; and the following year saw its completion with only one turnout from the main line and not two as in the 1844 plan. Also in 1845 the Birmingham and Gloucester Railway was taken over by the Midland Railway and construction began of the Oxford, Worcester and Wolverhampton Railway Company's branch line from Droitwich to Stoke Works Junction, this soon to be used not only for goods traffic, but also by employees travelling to and from Stoke Works.

The large-scale plan of 1844 for the branch line into the BAC is interesting as it shows the extent and the layout of both works in 1844. One feature of the plan is the inclusion of two terraces of houses, presumably for key workers, one on Shaw Lane by the railway bridge, known as Imperial Row, the other along the road over the Shaw Lane canal bridge, just beyond the chemical works and its tall chimney, known as British Row. There were ten three-storey houses in British Row and eight houses in Imperial Row and they remained in use and were not demolished until after World War Two.

Problems in the 1840s and their consequences

During the 1840s both manufacturing concerns maintained production of salt, chemicals and soap, but due to increasingly fierce competition, from Droitwich and from Cheshire, in the markets of London and other towns and cities, profits were low. Towards the end of the decade there were also problems due to the dilution in strength of the brine by seepage from the fresh-water springs into the wells. In 1845 the Worcester and Birmingham Canal Company, faced by railway competiton, reduced its tonnage on salt along the canal from 2 shillings to 1 shilling per ton. Other canal companies introduced similar drawbacks and this was some help. But towards the end of the decade the BAC and ISAC at Stoke Prior were both in financial difficulties. In 1845, to raise money, a mortgage of £12,000 on the property of the BAC at 5 per cent per annum was negotiated with John Fletcher. Eight years later, in 1853, Fletcher obtained powers for a receiver to be appointed to remit the 5 per cent interest directly to himself from John Corbett's rent on the lease of the works. It was probably the uncertain future of the BAC that led Gossage in 1850 to abandon the Stoke Prior Works and escape to Widnes.

In 1846 the finances of the BAC were put at risk when Francis Rufford signed an agreement with William Clay of the Droitwich Patent Salt Company for the BAC to lease the Droitwich Works for twenty-one years at a rent of £4,000 per annum. The Droitwich company, managed by Clay and Newman, had been struggling, and it seemed a good move at the time for the BAC to take over its chief local rival. Money was spent on plant at the Droitwich works but with little return, and in 1848/9 expensive action had to be taken by the BAC to prove and combat trespass by another firm who had tunnelled and laid a brine pipe under the property of their Droitwich works. There were legal wrangles and long delays in the drawing up of the lease which was never signed, and eventually in 1850, when a post-dated cheque for £4,000, one of several from Rufford's failing Bromsgrove Bank, was not met, the lease lapsed and Messrs Clay and Newman and the proprietors of their company had to salvage their business as best they could. One interesting outcome of the BAC's takeover of the Droitwich Works in 1846 was the provision by the BAC that year of rooms in Droitwich for night schools for male and female salt workers.

The financial affairs of the BAC were, as we have seen, very much in the hands of Francis Rufford. He was a man with various interests. There was the family firm, Heath Glass Works, near Stourbridge; two banks (Rufford and Wragge of Stourbridge and Rufford, Biggs & Co. of Bromsgrove); railways (he was a director of the Birmingham and Oxford, and the Birmingham and Wolverhampton Railways, and chairman by 1847 of the Oxford, Worcester and Wolverhampton Railway); he was a JP for the county of Stafford; and in 1847 he became MP for Worcester. Between 1842 and 1845 he had taken great interest, along with William Gossage, in the trials in Birmingham of disc steam engines on canal boats. Unfortunately, the investments of his banks on behalf of his depositors were not always wise, and in 1850 both banks failed and closed down. During bankruptcy proceedings against him in February 1852, he admitted that the Bromsgrove Bank, hoping for high interest, had embarked on insecure investments. The BAC owed the bank some £130,000 and he personally owed the bank thousands of pounds spent on his house (Yew Tree House, Belbroughton), on travelling, and on expenses incurred in his election as MP. He was declared bankrupt and in consequence had to resign his parliamentary seat; his house and various properties, including Stoke Corn Mill and the Bromsgrove Bank premises, were sold and he disappeared from public life. At the same time, William Gossage was being examined in the Liverpool Bankruptcy Court and the then whereabouts of Jonathan Fardon, whose home was at The Firs, Stoke Prior, were not known. With its three main directors in trouble, the BAC was by 1852 in deep financial difficulties. So also were many local people whose money had been lost in the collapse of Rufford's banks.

As for the ISAC, salt, vitriol and soda were its earliest products. From a report to the Court of Chancery in November 1850 on the company's affairs, we learn that within two or three years Richard Parker was replaced as manager, having cautioned some of the shareholders against paying more calls on their shares until they had investigated the firm's financial liabilities. Messrs Morrell then assumed direct control of the undertaking and Robert Morrell proceeded to apply the funds 'without check or control, employed builders and surveyors, and caused buildings to be erected for the manufacture of soap which were unnecessary'. By 1840 the shareholders had been informed that the £27,000 they had so far subscribed had been spent, that their bankers, Messrs Morrell, were owed £20,000, that other debts and liabilities amounted to £6,000, and that the company's patent 'for manufacturing soap out of flint' had proved a complete failure. During the 1840s no interest was paid to the shareholders and by the end of the decade the company owed its bankers over £90,000. Because of this and the fact that there was 'no properly constituted board of directors for carrying on the works' the company was put into the hands of receivers, and an official manager, William Turquand, was appointed to run it temporarily and wind up the company. In 1851 the works were offered for sale at the Auction Mart in London by Mr R Pike, under the direction of Turquand. The bill of sale was accompanied by a detailed plan showing three parts to the works:

(i) Salt works (at the southern end near the canal bridge), with six wooden steam-heated pans, twenty-five solid-fuel fired iron pans, brine tanks, drying stoves and warehouses,

(ii) Chemical works (adjoining the salt works to the north), with two lead vitriol chambers, pyrites furnaces, white and black ash and salt cake furnaces, boilers, engines and laboratory.

(iii) Soapery (adjoining the chemical works to the north again), with four 10-ton coppers, one 6-ton copper, mottled soap frames, engines, crystallising pans, iron vats and pumps.

These details do not mention the two brine pits of the ISAC, the older one to the north of the works being one of the pair originally sunk by MacAlister and still probably in use, and the newer one across the canal and close to the two pits of the BAC. Nor is there any mention of the rock-salt mine, initially created by Furnival in 1825 and situated a few yards away from the old brine pit, though it was still, apparently, in use around 1850, for *Slater's Worcestershire Directory* for that year lists the Imperial Salt and Alkali Company as also 'rock salt pit proprietors and manufacturing chemists', and an entry in the 1851 census return for Stoke Prior lists one Thomas Jones of Stoke Works as a salt miner. It is believed that the mine was soon discarded and filled in because the workings discoloured the brine pumped from the nearby well. The late Alf Nicklin knew a number of old saltworker pensioners in the 1950s who had been told by their predecessors about the existence of this rock-salt mine on the west bank of the canal near the railway bridge.

At the London auction the ISAC works were valued at upwards of £120,000, but there was no sufficient offer, so they were put up for sale by private treaty. They were eventually purchased by John Scott in 1853 at a knock-down price of £15,500 and continued in operation under the management of Richard Parker. In 1854 Scott mortgaged part of the property for over £16,000. He died at the end of that year, leaving a widow, a daughter and mortgaged works which closed down for a time. In June 1856 Parker was able to restart the works when Frank Clark Hills, a manufacturing chemist from Dartford in Kent, became the owner, taking over the mortgage and also paying £6,000 to Scott's daughter. It continued to trade as the Imperial Salt Company until 1858, when Hills leased it to John Corbett.

There is some doubt whether, after John Corbett obtained a lease of the BAC's works in 1852, the chemical and soap-making parts continued to be operated. Certainly by 1858 when Corbett became the owner of the BAC property, a map accompanying the agreement shows much of the chemical works dismantled and their site partly occupied by broad-salt panhouses. In 1854 and 1855 Henry Fowler Fardon, the son of Jonathan Fardon by his first

Three views of the works from the brine reservoir, looking from left to right and showing: (top) the woodyard and carpenters' shop in the foreground, steam-heated broad-salt panhouses beyond; (middle) the packing materials store with Belfast roof in the right foreground, fine-salt panhouses behind; (bottom) the old mill where salt lumps were sawn, offcuts ground, and salt was packed and dispatched.

wife Jane Fowler, is listed in trade directories under the heading Stoke Prior as a soap and salt manufacturer. However, this may be because he lived at The Firs, Stoke Prior, with his father Jonathan and stepmother. We know that some time after Jonathan Fardon came out to Stoke Prior in the late 1830s to set up his salt works one of his younger brothers, Joseph Ashby Fardon, took over a salt and chemical works at The Vines by the canal in Droitwich. In directories for 1851 and 1854 Joseph Ashby Fardon and Henry Fowler Fardon are listed as proprietors of one of eight salt works in Droitwich. So it seems that Henry was soap-making at the Droitwich Works and not at Stoke Works in the 1850s. Joseph Ashby Fardon remained as the sole proprietor at The Vines during the 1860s and at least until 1873. He died at the Willows, Droitwich, in 1876. Although the manufacture of chemicals and soap at Stoke Works was evidently not undertaken by John Corbett, it is possible that they continued to be produced by other people there, for as late as 1860 there is a reference in *Cassey's Directory of Worcestershire* to Eadon and Ingram of Stoke Prior, soap makers. It is known from the BAC's minutes of 1852 and 1853 that a John Ingram was renting a part of its property at Stoke Prior. In the 1858 map of Corbett's works, the soapery was still in situ, so soap might still have been made there or possibly in part of the old ISAC works.

The BAC continued in existence until 18 May 1859 when an extraordinary general meeting agreed to its winding-up and a final dividend of 4s 9d being paid on each of the 8,000 shares. By this time the BAC works had been acquired by John Corbett for a cash payment of £33,000 (in 1858), which enabled the company's debts to be paid as well as allowing the shareholders their final dividend.

Jonathan Fardon

It must have been somewhat galling for Jonathan Fardon to see the salt and chemical works, which he had started and built up and which had latterly fallen on bad times, pass into the hands of John Corbett and be so soon a business success. But perhaps he was glad to retire by 1852 and then to witness the survival of his salt works. He had been born in 1797 at Shipston-on-Stour, Gloucestershire, the son of Quaker parents, his father being a baker and miller with a shop in Shipston and a mill at Tredington two miles away. By 1823 he was married to Jane Fowler and living in Birmingham where his son Henry Fowler Fardon was born, and his business was then that of 'Flour Factor'. What caused him to be involved with salt production in Droitwich in 1824 remains a matter of conjecture. It was possibly through his Quaker connections, for, as reported in *Berrow's Worcester Journal* on 13 October 1825, the leading shareholders of the then newly-formed Droitwich Patent Salt Company were members of the Society of Friends. It may also have been connected with his marriage, for his wife Jane was the sister of Thomas Fowler, one of the Droitwich shareholders.

Fardon was evidently an enterprising, hard-working man, typical of other nineteenth-century Quaker founders of businesses. Following his retirement from the British Alkali Company in 1852, he experimented in making vinegar at his home in Stoke Prior, and around 1855 two of his sons by his second wife Deborah, Frederic and Alfred, moved to Birmingham and established a vinegar works in Bordesley. Fardon's Vinegar Company Limited, formed in 1860, continued in business under successive members of the Fardon family until its closure around 1960. The family's Quaker connection was severed when Jonathan Fardon, following the death of his first wife Jane in 1831, chose to marry his cousin Deborah, a practice forbidden under Quaker rules. It appears that some of Jonathan's six children by his second wife Deborah went to Stoke Prior School, for it is recorded that a local Quaker was a benefactor of the school.

Jonathan died at The Firs in 1858. As founder, director and manager of the British Alkali Company he had evidently been well respected by his employees, for in the possession of his great-grandson John Fardon are two interesting items, a silver two-handled presentation cup with the inscription 'presented to Jonathan Fardon Esq. by the workmen of the British Alkali Company as a testamony (sic) of their respect, August 1st. 1838', and an ornate Sheffield plate inkstand similarly inscribed.

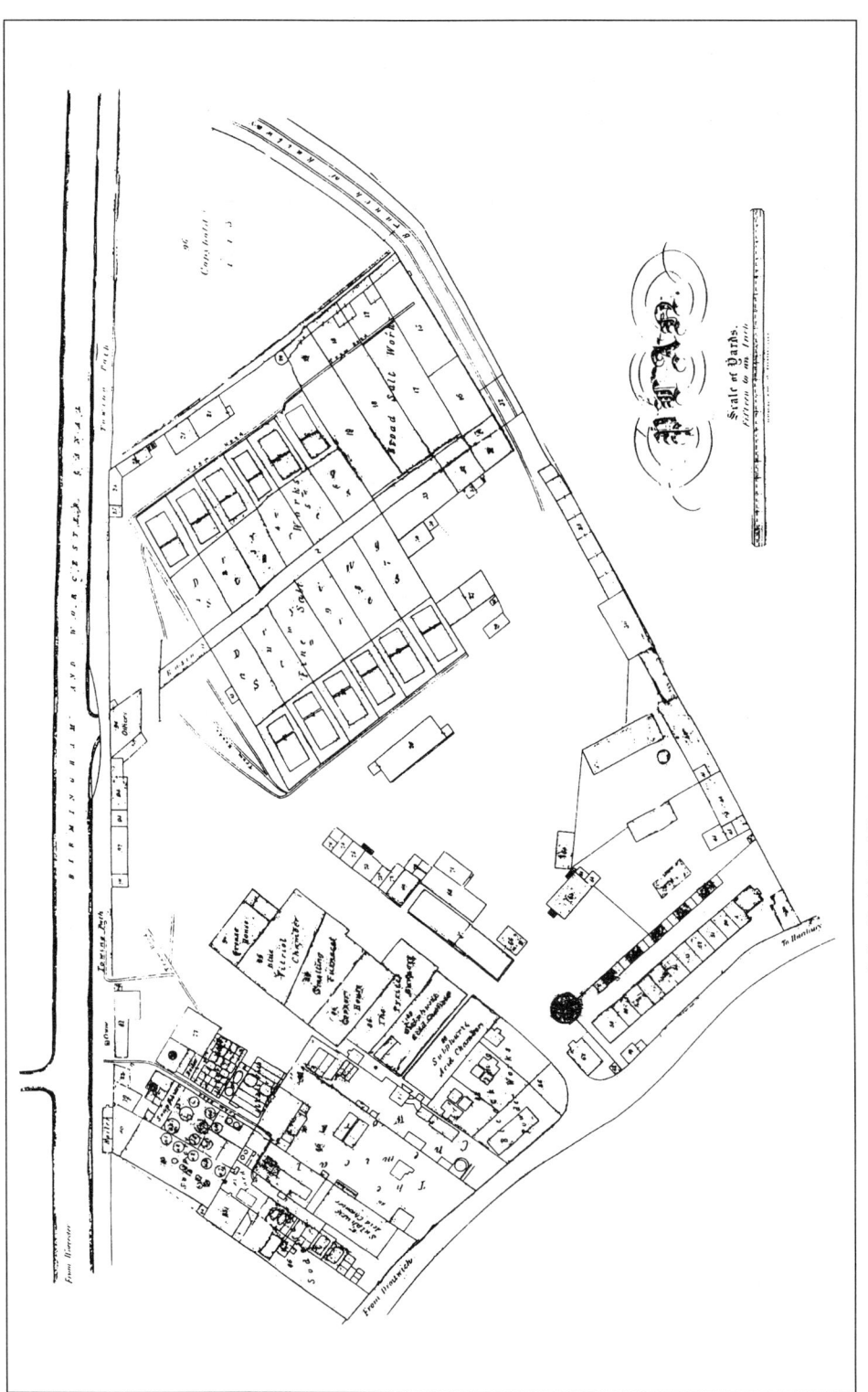

Plan of the British Alkali Works as leased to John Corbett in 1852.

Chapter 2

The Corbett Era: 1852-89

Takeover of the Stoke Works by John Corbett

By a legal agreement dated 9 March 1852, John Corbett was granted a 21-year lease of the British Alkali Company's works at a yearly rental of £2,500, payable half-yearly, commencing 1 January 1852. The indenture was signed by Henry Edward Beville and Joseph Pitman, directors of the BAC, as well as by John Corbett who is described as 'of Stoke Prior, Salt Merchant'. The twelve large pages of this interesting document include a detailed schedule of the land, brine springs, salt and chemical works, engines and ancillary plant, together with, on the last page, a large-scale plan of the works. A condition of the payment of full rental was that in any period of fourteen days enough brine could be pumped up to produce 600 tons of fine salt and 560 tons of broad salt.

The circumstances which led to John Corbett taking over the management of the BAC's works are far from clear, since Corbett himself apparently kept no diary or early records, nor did he explain how it came about in later interviews or in articles written about his salt works. Of his origins it is known that he was born in 1817 at Brierley Hill in the Black Country, where his father Joseph Corbett, formerly a Shropshire farmer, had set up a canal-carrying business. He was conceived out of wedlock but his mother Hannah Cole married Joseph on 13 April 1817 in Halesown parish church, two months before their child was born on 12 June. At the age of eleven young Corbett left school to join his father at his boatyard at Black Delph and to work on the boats. During the following years he travelled the canals and gained a great deal of knowledge of the canal network, the carrying business, canalside industries and the marketing of coal, timber and other commodities. His travels must have taken him to Stoke Works in which he took great interest, besides carrying salt and chemicals from there. In his obituary in the *Bromsgrove Messenger* (27 April 1901), it is stated that Corbett was twenty-eight years of age when he first became connected with the BAC. It was at this age, in the year 1845, that he became a commercial agent for the BAC at various places on the canal system, including London. The resident London agent of the company was Richard Westall of Thames Street, and Corbett is mentioned in a letter dated 2 April 1845 from Westall to Francis Rufford concerning canal tonnages and the price of salt in the London market. By the time he took over the BAC's works at the age of

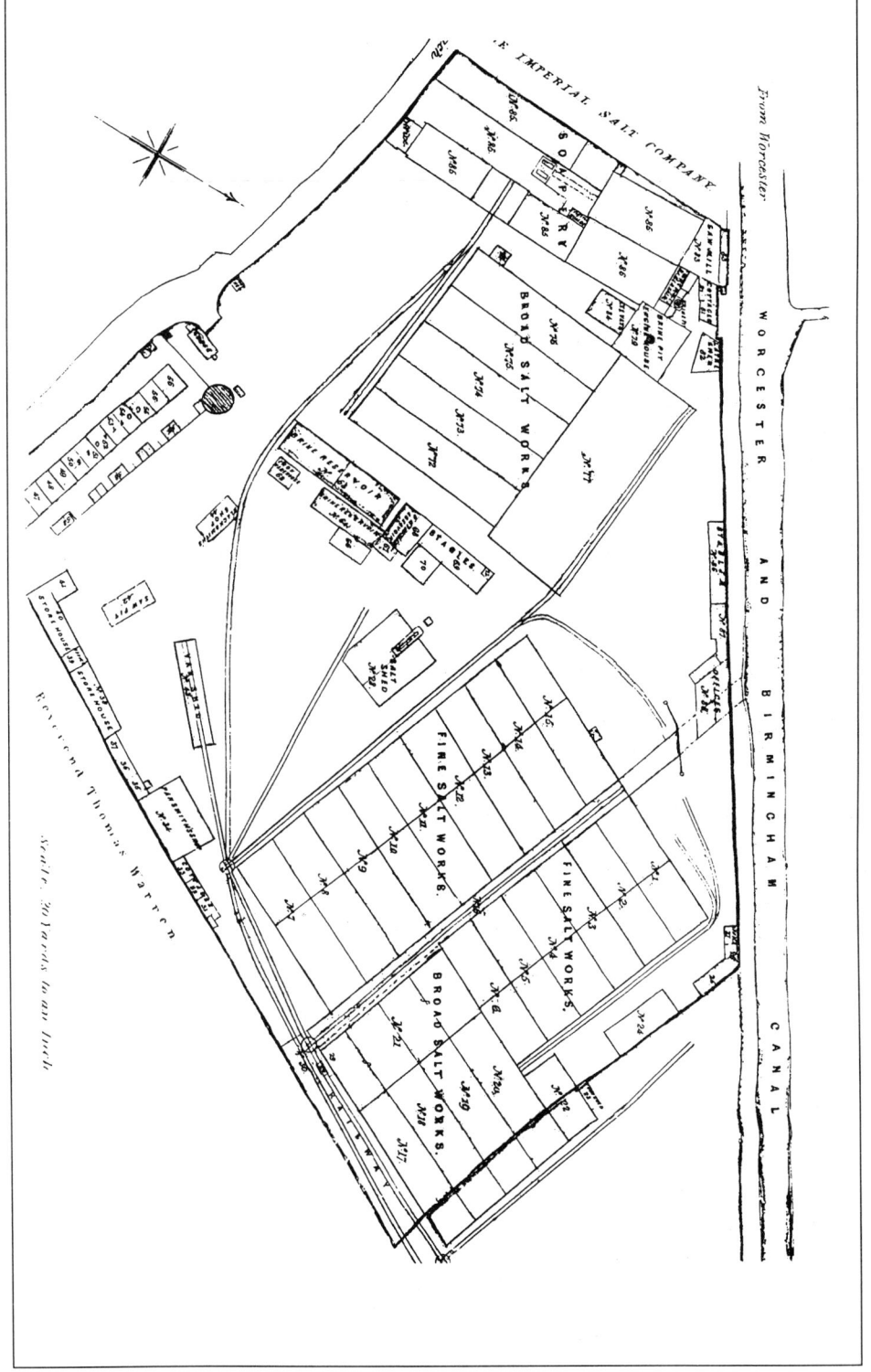

Plan of the British Alkali Works as purchased by John Corbett in 1858.

thirty-five, Corbett had long been a partner in his father's carrying business and also, as described in the 1852 lease indenture, a salt merchant.

Shrewd business man that he was, John Corbett would never have taken control of the BAC's salt works without considerable knowledge of the undertaking and a realisation of its potential and profitability if reorganised and developed. In the previous years he must have familiarised himself with its workings and its industrial and financial strengths and weaknesses. As both the BAC and the ISAC ran into financial problems around 1850, Corbett began to see his opportunity and to conceive plans for the future success of an expanded salt works without the chemical and soap-making sides which had been the least profitable parts of the enterprise. In his twenties he had spent some time as an apprentice at the Leys Ironworks in Stourbridge, where he acquired engineering skills and a working knowledge of steam engines, and this was to stand him in good stead. By 1852 canal carrying was facing increasing competition from the railways and John persuaded his father that the time had come to sell their joint business. With his share of the money Joseph retired. John's share was to be invested in the lease of the BAC, in developing the salt works and in buying adjacent land for investment and future expansion. It seems likely that by 1851 he had already had some experience of management within the works. At any rate, he was well prepared to take over the sole responsibility for the running of it by the beginning of 1852.

The works fire brigade, early 1920s. The building in the centre background, with clock and bellchamber above, contained the old offices, then still in use, over the canal arm into the works. Above the offices, on the first floor, John Corbett lived and slept when he took over the BAC's works in 1852. Of the firemen those identified are, from the left, 3rd Percy Mansell, 5th Albert Barrett, 6th Ernie Vaughan (captain), 7th Bill Clifford, 10th Harry Taylor.

An article entitled 'The Worcestershire Salt Works, Stoke Prior, near Droitwich', written in 1887 and published in *The Royal Album of Arts and Industries of Great Britain*, tells how, when John Corbett first leased the BAC plant, 'he slept over the offices on the Works, amid the smoke and steam, even descending the brine-pits from time to time when apparently unsurmountable difficulties appeared'. This tallies with the memories old salt workers handed down, that at the outset Corbett came and lived in the office building situated beside the canal towpath and above the canal arm into the salt works. He gathered round him a nucleus of men he could trust and together they set to work to restore the run-down salt works. He could not afford to pay them much, but later, when times were better, they were recompensed for their efforts.

One major problem which Corbett is believed to have faced initially was the dilution of the brine caused by fresh water seeping into the brine pits, which had been going on for some time and which experts, called in at great expense, had failed to solve. It was said that he solved this problem by lining the shafts with cast-iron cylinders with flanges bolted together and made watertight with a sealant. But this necessary lining of the pits had been done, as already mentioned, when they were first sunk. Corbett may well have had to deal with defects in the pit linings and the pumps, which is why he descended the pits himself on occasions.

From the outset, Corbett's real achievement was to produce the salt efficiently and economically and also to find new markets in which to sell it. When he took over in 1852, there had been several years of general business recession and times had been difficult but, fortunately, trade now began to revive and prices, including that of salt, began to rise. As an established salt merchant, he was soon able to make enough profit to maintain the lease, to begin to set up new broad-salt pans on the site of the chemical works, and to lease more land around his works in 1853 and 1854. His aim was to be the sole owner and proprietor of the business, but it was to be many years before the freehold of the land and premises of the former BAC, and later of the ISAC, were in his possession. Eventually, on 3 November 1857, an agreement was signed by four trustees of the BAC and by John Corbett for the latter to purchase the freehold of the Lower Leasow (the original BAC site of just over eight acres) and the copyhold of just over one acre of adjacent land bounded by the canal and the branch railroad into the works. The actual conveyance and financial settlement, although planned for 28 January 1858, was not made until 13 May, due to legal delays and the arranging, by John Corbett, of three mortgages on the property to help raise the purchase price of £33,000. The mortgages were for £12,000 loaned by Messrs Alger, Phelps, Kemp and Morris, for £10,000 loaned by Henry Summerfield and Edward Beville, and for £9,000 loaned by Thomas Wright and John Farmer. The third was paid off by Corbett in 1859; the other two, secured on the land and works leased in 1852, had to wait until 1866, under the terms of the lease, to be redeemed.

During the early years of Corbett's occupation of the BAC's works he was in competition with those who successively took over the former ISAC's works across the canal. Richard Parker, who had survived his earlier dismissal from the Imperial Company, continued to manage the works, first for John Scott

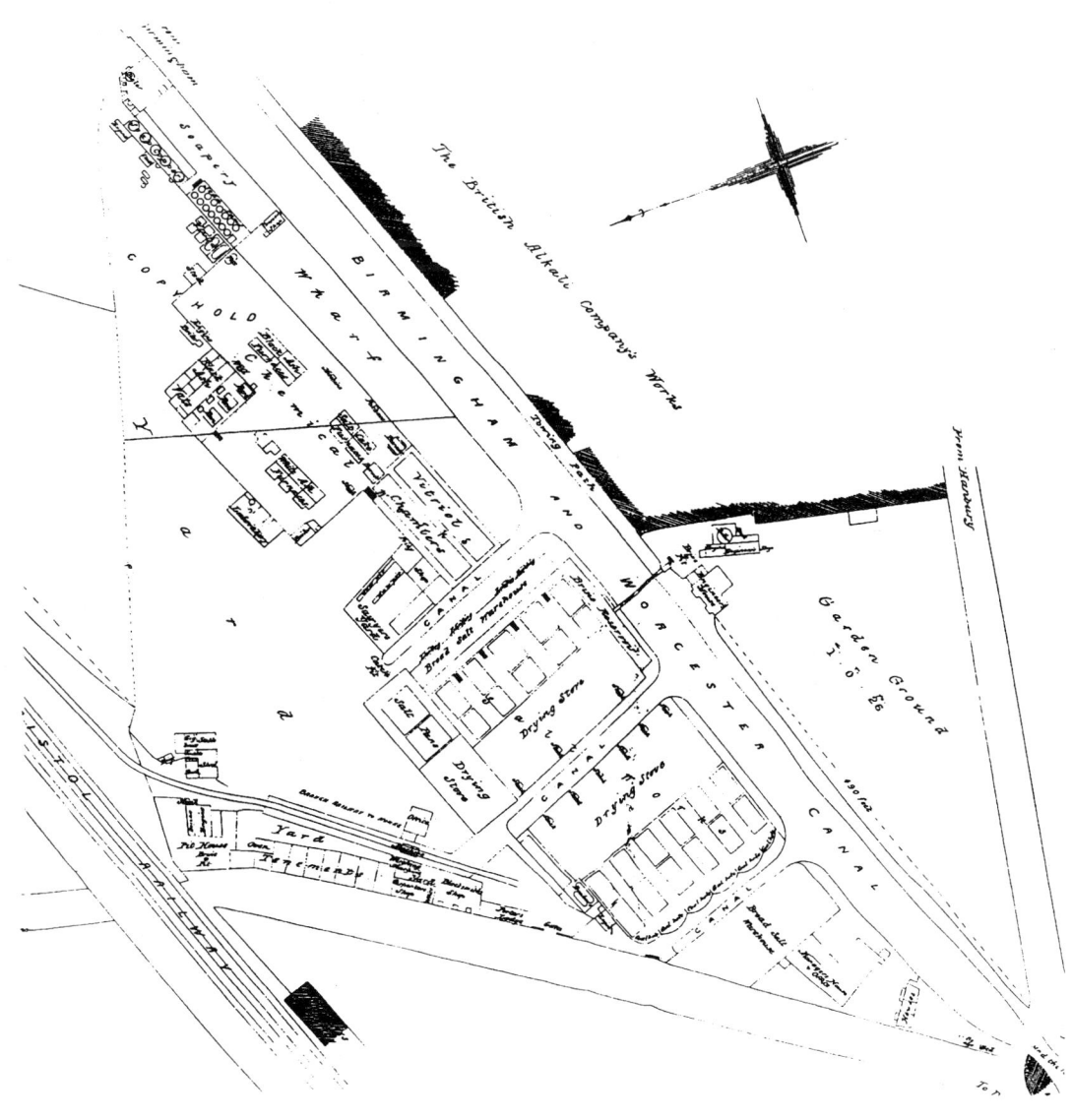

Detailed plan of the former ISAC salt and chemical works and soapery as leased by F C Hills to John Corbett in February 1858.

> Paid £25,500 –
> August 10 1867
>
> To John Corbett Esqre
> Stoke Prior
> Worcester
>
> I hereby authorise and request you to pay to my Solicitors, Messrs Pattison, Wigg & Co of 50, Lombard Street, £25,500 being the purchase money mentioned in the document signed by me
>
> Your obedient Servant,
>
> F. C. Hills

Agreement and receipt by which John Corbett finally purchased the former ISAC works from F C Hills on 10 August 1867 and thus became the owner of the entire Stoke Prior Salt Works.

from 1853 to 1854 and then for F C Hills who, some time after Scott's death in December 1854, became the new owner. Parker was a tough competitor and his method of picking up business by undercutting Corbett and the Droitwich producers led Corbett to enlist the aid of some of the latter in his plan to buy out the ex-Imperial business. After some hard bargaining, Corbett was able to come to an agreement with Hills to lease his works from 25 February 1858 for a period of twenty-one years at £1,800 per annum with an option to purchase for £25,500. To satisfy Parker and get him out of the way, Corbett agreed to pay him an annuity of £750 on condition that he would never again engage in the salt trade, Parker being liable to a penalty of £15,000 if he did so. It was nine years later, in 1867, that Corbett was able to exercise his option to purchase the former ISAC works from Hills for £25,500. He was now the owner and sole proprietor of the whole Stoke Works complex. His ambition had been achieved.

Corbett's marriage and family

The prosperity of Corbett's business empire was dependent partly on the high quality of his salt which he took all possible steps to maintain, and partly on his energy and enterprise in marketing it. Within a year or so of setting up business, he was able to leave the works in the hands of trusted managers and foremen and to travel far afield in the search for new markets. It was on one of these trips that in 1855 in Paris he met Anna Eliza O'Meara, one of the two daughters of William O'Meara, Secretary of the Diplomatic Corps, from whom he was seeking information and advice about business contacts. He fell in love with her, and they were married the following year in the French capital. Their first home, from 1856 to 1862, was at Rigby Hall, Finstall, which was then in the parish of Stoke Prior. This was some three miles from Stoke Works and Corbett could have travelled up and over Buntsford Hill to the works in his own horse-drawn vehicle or, conveniently, by train between Bromsgrove Station near his home and Stoke Works Station. In October 1862 Rigby Hall was put up for sale. By this time the Corbetts had three young daughters and, with their six servants, they decided to move to a more convenient home, Stoke Grange (now Avoncroft College), at Stoke Heath, less than a mile away from Stoke Works.

Anna Eliza had been born and brought up in Paris. Her father was Irish; her mother Eliza was French. Well-educated and talented, she was fifteen years younger than her husband and she was a Roman Catholic, whereas he was a staunch member of the Church of England. However, in spite of these differences, they seem to have got on together in the earlier years of their marriage and by 1866 they had five children, Mary Eliza, Camille Anna, Kathleen Hannah, John Roger and Walter John, whose respective ages at the census of 2 April 1871 were 14, 11, 10, 7 and 5 years. Having had three daughters to begin with, John Corbett must have been glad to have had two sons, hoping, no doubt, that at least one of them would in time join him and eventually take over his salt works. But in this he was to be disappointed. For several years, around 1860, Thomas B O'Meara, Anna Eliza's slightly older

The three Worcestershire homes of John Corbett: Rigby Hall 1856-62; Stoke Grange 1862-72; Impney Hall (Chateau Impney) c.1877-1901.

brother, was employed at the works as a cashier. He lived with his wife Marie Camille and their three young childen at The Firs, formerly the home of Jonathan Fardon.

Corbett's Stoke Prior Salt Works

It is interesting to compare the BAC plant which Corbett took over in 1852 with that of his extensive salt works in its heyday around 1880. Contemporary descriptions of the latter are to be found in Littlebury's 1879 *Directory of Worcestershire* and in William Curzon's book *The Manufacturing Industries of Worcestershire* (1881). In 1852 the BAC works covered just over nine acres of land. In 1880 the works extended over thirty acres. Corbett took over two brine pits from the BAC, but at the time one was out of action. That in use was in a 'pit house' which also housed a 16 h.p. disc steam engine, with boiler, air pump and condensing apparatus, working an 8-inch pump, having all beams, wheels and gearing complete. For the other pit there was an engine house containing a 12 h.p. high-pressure engine with boilers, wheels and gearing complete. By 1880 there were four brine pits in use, the extra pair having belonged to the ISAC, one being the original MacAlister pit, the other Reid and Parker's on the east side of the canal. The old BAC pits were 3 feet in diameter and about 200 feet deep; the newer Imperial pit nearby, reconstructed in 1878, was 6 feet in diameter and 250 feet deep. From the bottom of each pit shaft a pipe of about 3 inches in diameter was sunk several hundred feet further down to the level of the brine source. Each pump was situated at the bottom of its shaft just above the level to which the brine naturally rose.

To store the brine pumped up, there were in 1852 three brine reservoirs in the midst of the BAC site, one raised on brick pillars. In the 1870s Corbett constructed a large brine reservoir, with a brick lining, on the hillside facing his works. This open reservoir had a capacity of some 400,000 gallons, sufficient for about ten days supply, the salt pans being filled and replenished by gravity feed through a network of pipes. A watch was kept upon the brine reservoir to prevent vandalism and pollution. A smaller freshwater reservoir was constructed nearby to serve the works, this being filled from freshwater springs by means of a wind pump.

In 1852 the BAC's works included twelve fine-salt panhouses, each containing two fine-salt pans 20 to 25 feet long by about 20 feet wide and varying in depth from about 1 foot to 2 feet 6 inches. To each of these panhouses there were three furnaces which, besides heating the pans, also heated the drying stoves through brick flues to the smoke stack. Eight of the panhouses, numbered 5-12, had direct access to a tramroad situated above the canal tunnel arm so that the fine-salt lumps could be directly loaded into railway wagons. The salt could also be loaded directly, through manholes and down shutes, into canal boats. Besides this group of fine-salt panhouses, there were four much larger broad-salt panhouses. Each contained two broad-salt pans, one pair being 90 feet by 14 feet and 2 feet 8 inches deep, other pairs 150 to 155 feet long, 14 feet wide, and only about 1 foot 3 inches deep. Two of these broad-salt panhouses used the direct heat from furnaces, the other two used steam heat. Attached were broad-salt warehouses where the salt was stacked loosely, dried and either bagged or else loaded loose into carts, wagons or canal boats. Other buildings included a pansmiths' shop, carpenters' shop, stabling for ten horses, various tenements, including a 'School House now used by Mr. Hunt for Divine Service'. The chemical works were quite extensive, and the soapery contained eleven soap coppers of from 5 to 35 tons, 65 patent cast-iron soap frames and soap-cutting machinery.

By his takeover of the ISAC works, which had about twenty-five coal-fired iron saltpans and six wooden steam-heated broad-salt pans Corbett must have doubled his salt-producing capacity. This was further increased by the building of broad-salt panhouses on the chemical works sites of both the British and Imperial Works and also on land bought on the northern perimeter of the BAC site. Then in 1871/2, at a cost of some £30,000, new works, with a siding from the Midland Railway, were built for the installation of patent 'machine pans', of a type already in use in several salt works in Cheshire, together with ancillary plant. Contrary to what was generally believed, John Corbett was not the inventor of these patent pans. The only patent ever taken out by him was in 1860 (no. 1135) for evaporating pans made of cast-iron plates with flanges bolted together (instead of the usual wrought-iron plates rivetted together), and with troughs at the edges into which the salt was to be raked and from which brine could drain back into the pan through small holes. As far as is known such pans were never actually made and used.

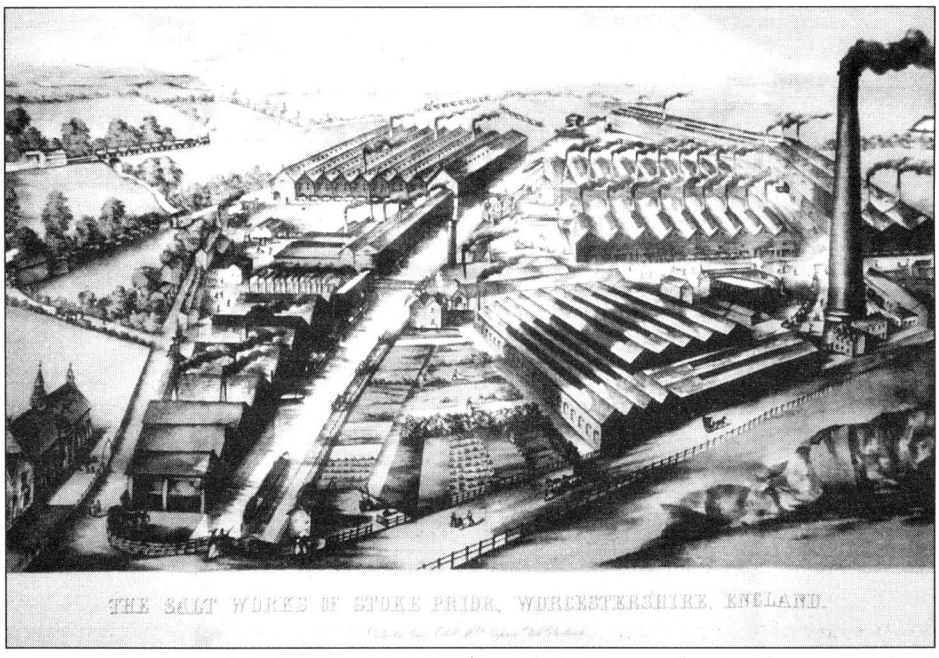

A print depicting John Corbett's extensive salt works circa 1875. His new school, bottom left, was included, though actually further down Shaw Lane. Bottom right is the claypit of his brickworks.

The machine pans, which produced a superior quality of dense fine salt, were circular, about 20 feet in diameter, with conical covers to retain the steam. Each was heated by three furnaces. Inside each pan were a number of stirrers and scrapers on arms which revolved mechanically about a central vertical spindle powered from above. The agitation of the brine, and the greater heat caused by the retention of the steam (which in the case of the open pan was wasted) combined to cause a rapid depositing of salt, and the crystals were consequently very fine and hard. The crystalised salt was forced out through an opening in the side of each pan by centrifugal motion and by the paddles into a trough rivetted to the side of the pan, and then either ladled into tubs to produce squares which were dried in a special stove 120 feet long, or else dried loose in a nearby warehouse and sold as butter salt. Some of the squares were carefully ground and packed in jars or cartons and sold as the finest table salt; others were sawn into cut lumps and packed in boxes for export. The steam from the patent pans was piped off to heat nearby broad-salt pans.

Every salt works needed skilled maintenance staff, foundrymen, rivetters and others for the constant repair and renewal of the pans due to corrosion; engineers, blacksmiths and fitters to repair and maintain machinery, engines and pumps; and plumbers, carpenters and bricklayers to maintain the buildings. So Corbett took over various workshops on both the British and Imperial sites, including pansmiths', carpenters' and plumbers' shops, and he developed and improved these facilities. His policy was to become self-sufficient in other directions also. By 1860 he had established a brickworks on land on the east side of the canal below Shaw Lane Bridge, now the site of the Social Club and car park. Clay was plentiful here, as at many other locations along the Worcester and Birmingham Canal. The bricks and tiles produced by Corbett were used not only for extending his works, but also for the building of houses and facilities for his workpeople. Some of the bricks bearing the imprint of his name are preserved in the Droitwich Heritage Centre and at Avoncroft Museum of Buildings. The brickworks seems to have closed by the time Corbett sold out to the Salt Union in 1889, and the site with its claypit was used for many years as a tip for the disposal of rubbish and nightsoil from the village privies.

Corbett's boatyard, canal boats, and use of railways

Over the years from 1846 to 1876, a boat-builder named Samuel Shellard was listed in directories of Worcestershire as being in business at Stoke Works. The site of his boatyard was on the west side of the canal just north of the BAC's railway bridge, and since he lived with his wife Ann and children in British Row he was evidently employed by the BAC which owned some boats and employed its own boat crews, as did the ISAC. Employed by Samuel Shellard in the early years were probably Robert Archer of Stoke Pound and Henry Spencer of Stoke Works, both boat-builders. It was natural that Corbett, with his knowledge and experience of boat-building and canal-carrying in the family business, should want to build up his own fleet of canal boats, both for the collection of coal and the distribution of his salt. By the 1870s there were over fifty boats registered in his name, and Samuel Shellard must have been kept busy both building and servicing them. When Shellard retired in 1876, Corbett invited two brothers, George and Joseph Farrin from Flore in Northamptonshire, to take over the boatyard. He provided each of them with one of his workers' cottages in Stoke Works Village. George, aged thirty-six, his wife Sarah and daughter Florrie, moved into 4 Shrubbery Terrace. Joseph, aged twenty-nine, his wife Mary and children Tom and Gertrude moved into 14 Sagebury Terrace. They were to run the boatyard, assisted by Tom after he left school at the age of twelve, for many many years, long after the Corbett era, and into the 1920s, and they and their families were long involved with the new Wychbold Church, George, Joseph and Tom as choristers, and Florrie as the organist there.

The Canal Boats Act of 1877 required all canal boats on which the crew slept to be registered. The first register of the Birmingham Sanitary Authority, started in 1879, lists forty-five such boats that year owned by John Corbett. These were all engaged in taking salt in the London direction via the Grand Union Canal, and in bringing coal back to Stoke. Some carried sand and chalk back from the London area, under contract, to Chance Brothers' Chemical Works, Oldbury, to which Corbett also supplied industrial salt. Two-thirds of the masters of these well-used boats lived locally; of the remainder almost all came from Braunston, a busy canal village situated at the junction of the Grand Union and Northern Oxford Canals near Daventry. Other boats took salt to Worcester and down the Severn to Gloucester, either to the docks to be transshipped to ocean-going vessels or to the warehouse taken over by Corbett from the BAC in 1855. These boats were probably registered with the Worcester Sanitary Authority, but unfortunately the early records of this body seem to have been lost or destroyed.

John Corbett's motives in making extensive use of canal transport were stated in a letter to Chance Brothers of Oldbury in 1874: 'I am desirous as an old Canal carrier (and my father before me) to keep a fair portion of my trade on the water as a wholesome check on railway companies.' He was a director of the Worcester and Birmingham Canal until its takeover in 1874 by the Sharpness New Docks and Birmingham Navigation Company and he had maintained cordial relations with the old company. But he was soon in trouble with the new company when, in 1875, he discharged salt water into the canal and killed many fish. His principal pit had failed, probably due to seepage into it of spring water, and to restore it he had to pump out the top water, impregnated with salt, into the canal. Corbett maintained that this practice had been allowed in the past; he claimed a traditional 'right of easement'; and he argued that the death of fish was a lesser evil than the closure of the works which would have resulted in a loss of several thousand pounds per annum to the canal company.

Besides depending upon water transport, John Corbett also made good use of the railways. Some five miles of railway track and tramroad served his works, enabling coal to be delivered direct to the furnaces and boilers and salt

John Corbett's wagon works which continued in use under the Salt Union. Here railway wagons and vans were made and repaired.

Various types and packages of salt produced by the Salt Union at Stoke Prior. The Black Horse was one of Corbett's trademarks, used by his London agents.

to be loaded from inside the works. Two 0-4-0 steam locomotives, *Elephant* and *Raven*, pulled and pushed wagons and vans along the main sidings; horses were used for haulage on the branch tramways. By the 1870s and 1880s John Corbett owned around 700 vans and wagons carrying his name, and he had a large well-equipped wagon shop where his vans and wagons were made and repaired. Records of these vehicles, their tare (unladen) weights, their loadings and their movements on the rail network had to be carefully kept. The wagon shop continued in use later under the Salt Union and the ICI until its closure in 1950.

Ending of female labour in the salt works

John Corbett inherited a system of labour, as described by Dr Hastings in 1835 and still practised in 1852, under which contractors were allotted salt pans to manage and were paid by results, according to the amount of salt produced. The contractors employed what labour they needed, including members of their families, for a weekly wage. There were no set hours and women worked and sweated alongside the men, lading and moving the salt in the hot steamy atmosphere of the panhouses, wearing a minimum of clothing, and often bedding down, living on the job from early Monday morning to Saturday afternoon. For some years Corbett allowed this system to continue but as a respectable member of the Church of England, holding high moral principles, he eventually took drastic action and towards the end of 1859 stopped the

The brass plaque in the chancel of St Michael's Church, Stoke Prior, stating that the east window was inserted in 1860 by some friends of John Corbett 'to commemorate his having nobly stood forward in the cause of Morality by putting an end to the employment of female labour at his Salt Works in this Parish'.

employment of female labour in his works. To compensate families for the wife's loss of earnings he increased the wages of the men and improved their conditions by introducing a direct-management structure and a double-shift system. The result was improved efficiency, and the men were able to spend more time at home with their families. So impressed were the local gentry at this moral step that in 1860 they had a stained-glass window put in the east end of Stoke Prior Church and a brass plaque on the nearby chancel wall to commemorate the event.

John Corbett was by no means a pioneer in the abolition of female labour in his salt works, this having taken place in Cheshire a number of years earlier. But it was a bold step in Worcestershire, and Corbett tried, unsuccessfully, to persuade his fellow salt proprietors in Droitwich to follow his lead. In 1861 Mr F Zachary of Stourport, a director of one of the Droitwich companies, received the following letter, dated 23 June, from John Corbett:

My dear Sir,
I am only just returned from London and find your note of the 20th. inst.

It is some satisfaction to me to inform you that the movement I made in December 1859, in regard to the non-employment of female labour in my works at Stoke Prior, has been attended with success.

The families attend to their domestic duties and save more money to their families than they earned in the Salt Works — they often — to the Rector of the Parish — express themselves delighted with the reformations, and state that they would be sorry to return to the former comparative state of degradation. I take the liberty of expressing my opinion in the form of two or three remarks in regard to the applicability of the same reformation in Droitwich.

1st. I believe the moral condition in regard to the employment of females at Droitwich is no better than it formerly was at Stoke, and that as much immorality exists.

2nd. As I have before stated, the females are more profitably employed in their domestic duties, and the fear of their being prejudiced by being thrown out of employment is not likely to have serious results.

3rd. There is not only a moral satisfaction in abolition, but a pecuniary saving.

4th. Droitwich — so far as I know — is the only place at which female labour is employed in Salt Works.
Believe me, Dear Sir,
Yours faithfully,
John Corbett.

The Droitwich works did not cease to employ women salt workers, although by about 1870 they were no longer employed at night. One of the last women salt workers at Droitwich worked for many years for Boucher and Giles from 6.00 am to 6.45 pm on weekdays and until 3.00 pm on Saturdays. Her pay was 10 shillings per week; she wore a calico 'shimmy' and a calico skirt. Interviewed in 1956 she said: 'We did everything, tapped the squares, run 'em in the stove, worked the pan, and filled the tubs, just like a man.' She sometimes fired the pan when the fireman was drunk. 'They brought them little trams to run the salt in the stoves, then they stopped we women.' This seems to have occurred around 1905.

Recognising the manual dexterity of women in the packaging of salt, Corbett did eventually employ them in this department, but they were entirely segregated from the men and protected from male molestation.

Corbett's provisions for, and expectations of, his employees

Like some other enlightened employers in the latter part of the nineteenth century, Corbett felt it to be his Christian duty to improve the living conditions, the health and the moral and spiritual state of his workpeople. By around 1870 his finances were in a very healthy state, he had become a substantial local landowner, and he had plans to build a large multipurpose school and many tied houses for his employees in Stoke Works Village.

The foundation stone of the new school was laid by his young son Roger on 25 October 1871. Costing £2,000, it was built by his own workmen and took less than a year to complete, and it was officially opened by the Bishop of Worcester on 12 August 1872. The gothic-style building incorporated a lecture hall 90 feet by 36 feet which could be partitioned into two rooms, a class room 12 feet by 36 feet, an infants school 22 feet by 30 feet and it was intended for up to 500 children. There was a large playground and a schoolhouse attached. The building was licenced by the bishop for divine service, and furnished with an American organ bearing the inscription 'Presented to the workpeople of Stoke Works by Thomas Weston, of London, for use in the new schools, 1872'. (Thomas Weston was one of the partners in Weston and Westall, 115 Lower

John Corbett's Stoke Works School, built 1872. It was used as a church on Sundays until Wychbold Church was built. It also housed a dispensary. At the far end is the schoolmaster's house.

Thames Street, London, Corbett's London agents). On the day of the opening, Mr and Mrs Corbett were presented with various gifts by the workpeople and their wives, the event reported in the *Bromsgrove Messenger*:

> ... they entertained a distinguished party at Impney on the occasion, including the Bishop, the Lord Lieutenant, Baron Amphlett, the Hon C.G.Lyttelton, and others; and in the evening of the same day upwards of 500 of Mr. Corbett's workpeople and neighbours were entertained at a sumptuous dinner by him in the new buildings; the children of the schools were also entertained in a manner befitting the occasion. On the following day also the wives of the workpeople and others, to the number of 700, were entertained at tea in the new lecture hall by Mrs. Corbett.

Stoke Works School continued to serve the village well for over one hundred years, until its closure at the end of 1986. However, shorn of its original pinnacles and clock, it continues to be used for educational purposes as the John Corbett Centre.

At about the same time as his school was built, Corbett erected Sagebury Terrace on the south side of it. This was a row of fifty-six substantial dwellings with long back gardens stretching to the railway. They had outside privies and no running water. Drinking water could be obtained from a large fountain by the road over Shaw Lane Bridge, or from several cast-iron fountains in Shaw Lane. Tap water was not installed until 1929. Other houses were also provided in the village, including Shrubbery Terrace backing onto the canal. Workpeople

Inscription in John Corbett's handwriting in a large Bible presented by him to Samuel Paxton, one of his employees, at the opening of Stoke Works School and Lecture Hall, 12 August 1872.

and their families continued to occupy these houses until they were demolished in the early 1970s. For many of the occupants it was sadly the end of an era and the splitting up of a community with its roots in the salt works.

Other ways in which Corbett benefitted his employees are set out in an 'addenda' to the edition of the Rules and Regulations issued by him to his workmen in 1872:

> I.– The workmen on Stoke Works shall be entitled to receive from the Storekeeper a ticket for two hundredweight of coal per week, for which they shall pay the cost price and railway carriage, as fixed for the time being; but no workman shall be allowed to accumulate his tickets, to sell his coal, or to draw more than two hundredweight per week.
>
> II.– Schools for children of workmen are provided, under able teachers.
>
> III.– Lectures and Penny Readings will be held in the large School-room from time to time.
>
> IV.– Divine Service will be celebrated in the School-room every Sunday, by a Clergyman provided by Mr. Corbett.
>
> V.– A Dispensary is provided on the establishment, where drugs and medicines of the best quality will constantly be provided for the workmen and their families. A Surgeon will attend at the Dispensary at fixed hours on certain days of the week, and in certain special cases — where the patients from a distance, or otherwise, are unable to walk — at their own homes.

In addition to these benefits, Corbett provided each year a gift of 'Christmas Beef' to the families of his workpeople, a custom which was continued by the Salt Union until 1912. He also supported the establishment, in July 1877, of a workmen's club in what had formerly been the George Inn.

John Corbett continued to arrange for church services each Sunday in the school, until the church of St Mary de Wyche at nearby Wychbold was built. He contributed generously to the cost of this new church which was opened on 31 August 1888. For non-Anglicans there was a small Wesleyan Methodist Chapel on the works site next to British Row, in the building that had once been a schoolhouse.

The relationship between Corbett and his workpeople was one of benevolent dictatorship. He was a strict disciplinarian and, provided they obeyed the rules and gave of their best, they enjoyed wages some 10 to 15 per cent above those in other salt works. His 'Rules and Regulations' included the giving of a fortnight's notice by the proprietor or by an employee of termination of employment, but instant dismissal for drunkenness, neglect of work, dishonesty, disobeying the orders of the manager or foremen, or any unruly or unseemly conduct. To maintain the efficiency of production and the quality of his product, Corbett included the following advice and exhortation:

> X.– Considerable loss has been sustained both by masters and men through carelessness in allowing pans to be burnt — to the master in the stoppage of the

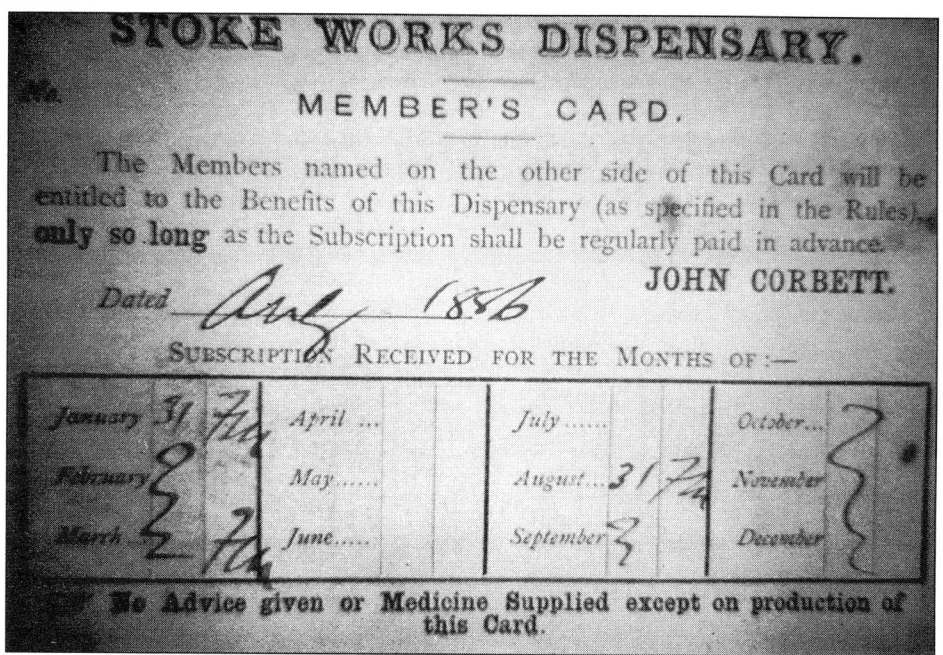

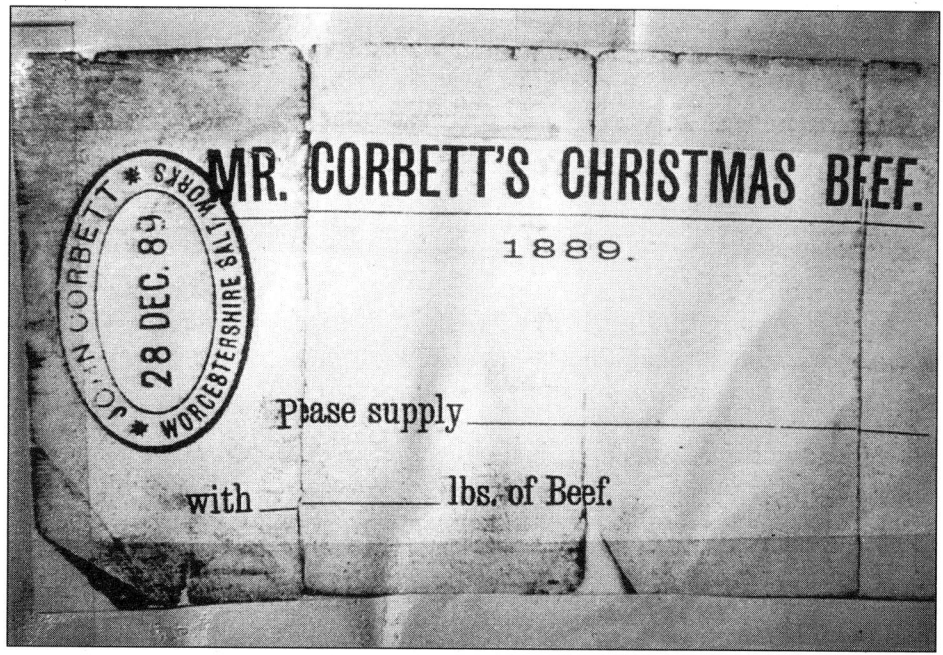

Two ways in which John Corbett benefitted his employees and their families, but he expected a contribution towards the cost of the dispensary in his school, perhaps in the belief that it would, in consequence, be more highly valued and not taken for granted and abused.

Works and repairs, and to the men in the loss of the make of Salt whilst the Works are under repair. I trust that every Saltmaker will do justice to himself and his employer by taking every care of his pan.

XI.– I am most desirous that every Saltmaker — Fine and Broad — should get good wages, but that, of course, will depend upon themselves, and the quality of Salt produced at each and every Work; and I do hope and trust that no time will be lost. Every Fine Salt Work will, at the latest, be expected to be in full operation at four o'clock on every Monday morning. I am induced to hope that every Fine Saltmaker will, for his own credit and the reputation of Works, take a pride in turning out Salt of good colour, and thereby maintain the good name these Works have enjoyed for so many years for the quality and colour of the Salt they produce.

XII.– All doors to be shut at Fine, Broad, and Butter Salt Works when slack is being unloaded or ashes being got out, or loaded. A fine for each and every offence of the infringement of this rule.

XIII.– All ashes, before being loaded into carts, must be watered, to prevent the dust flying into the Salt Works and damaging the Salt, under a fine for each offence.

In addition to these rules, Corbett issued occasional homilies in the form of little booklets. One, issued in January 1878, was entitled *A Few Words of Friendly Counsel to the Workmen at Stoke Prior Salt Works*; another, dated January 1882, was headed *A Few Words to the Workpeople at Stoke Prior Salt Works*. Both began by bemoaning the depressed and profitless state of the salt trade. In the first Corbett extolled the success of his 'Model Salt Works of England' and the benefits enjoyed by his workforce, and called upon them to rally round and accept some restraints on wages 'till the storm be over and better times come around'. He warned against trade union agitators and the damage and suffering caused by strike situations he had seen during a recent visit to America. In Cheshire many saltworkers had been laid off, but he had kept many men on in labouring jobs rather than put them out of work. There was a plea not to waste coal and to maintain the colour and quality of the salt. Finally, he wrote: 'After your work is done, I wish you to have rational recreation and enjoyment in any reasonable degree, consistent with good morals and temperance. At the same time, I hope you will not neglect what you owe to your Maker, and that you will attend to your religious duties.'

The 1882 epistle reflected a gloomier outlook, 20,000 to 30,000 tons of salt (about two months output) in store, pans out of commission, and prices low due to over-production and foreign competition. A similar appeal for care and loyalty was followed by a four-page sermonette on the need for Christian charity and goodwill, family loyalties, temperance, thrift and honesty in word and deed, respect for authority and a caution against agitators in the workplace. Both booklets reflect the current problems then facing the salt industry and the threat of trade union infiltration and intervention. One wonders to what extent Corbett's moral and spiritual exhortations were taken seriously.

Travels and awards

Over the years John Corbett travelled overseas on numerous occasions in connection with his business and also for pleasure. From his business letters, 1870-78, we know he was in Belgium early in 1871 where the government had abolished its country's import duty on salt, and he was considering the possibility of building a steamer to export salt from the Lincolnshire port of Boston to Antwerp. In January 1872 he visited the Continent and Egypt. In December 1872 he was in France with his children and stayed in the Villa des Cedres, Pau, in Basses Pyrenees. In 1877 he went to America with his sons and stayed in New York.

Corbett had a considerable volume of export trade in salt and his reputation was enhanced by awards gained at various exhibitions worldwide. By 1880 gold medals had been gained at exhibitions in London, Paris, Philadelphia, Sydney and Melbourne for the general superiority of his salt in colour and purity, the awards given for all classes, including table salt, fine- or coarse-grained broad salt, bay salt, fishery salt, and butter salt. The salt was mostly shipped abroad from the ports of Gloucester and Bristol in bags bearing Corbett's trademark, a castle on an elephant, or from London by his agents, Messrs Weston and Westall, under the trademark of a black horse.

Public figure and benefactor

John Corbett was an ambitious man, keen not only to make a success of his salt works, but also to make his mark in public life, and achieve fame and recognition. In 1864 he became a JP for Worcestershire. He set up in politics as a Liberal and in 1868 contested the Droitwich parliamentary seat against Sir John Packington of Westwood House, whose family had held it for the Tories for many years. On this occasion Corbett was defeated, but in 1874 he was successful, and he remained an MP until the dissolution of Parliament in 1892. He contributed £50,000 to Liberal Party funds but, as Corbett himself remarked in later years, Mr Gladstone never said so much as 'thank you'. In fact Corbett made little impact as a politician.

Over the years Corbett contributed a great deal of money to institutions and causes, many of which had local or family connections. In 1873 he had two stained-glass windows put into St Michael's Church, Brierley Hill, in memory of his parents who were buried in the churchyard there, and he later defrayed the cost of a new east window. In 1886 he built at his own expense a Mission Church at Delph, scene of his Black Country boyhood. He gave most, if not all, of the money needed to build the new church of St Mary de Wyche at Wychbold near to his works. He became the patron of the living of Dodderhill, and the church, which overlooked the town of Droitwich and which had been damaged by subsidence, was restored by him in 1890, and stained-glass windows put in, at a cost of over £3,000. He gave £4,500 for the repair and restoration of the parish church of St Michael, Stoke Prior, completed in 1895. He also gave generously to many other appeals for churches and cathedrals.

He agreed to be president of the committee formed in 1877 to build a Cottage Hospital in Bromsgrove, and he continued in this office until his death, subscribing in a major way to the first hospital in Alcester (now Stratford) Road, and its successor in New Road. He also bought a mansion, The Hill, and its grounds at Amblecote, near Stourbridge, in 1892 and gave £2,500 towards its conversion into the eighteen-bed Corbett Hospital which opened in 1893.

The town of Droitwich benefitted greatly from his interest and generosity. He was elected an honorary member of the Salters Company in 1879 and that same year started the building of the Salters Hall in Droitwich which opened in 1881. Capable of seating 1,500 people, it was a great asset to the people of the town for meetings, lectures and concerts, but it remained his property. He eventually owned about half the area of the town, including the brine rights; he provided the park, he acquired and developed the Raven Hotel, he built the Worcestershire Brine Baths Hotel, and also converted another property into the Elephant and Castle Hotel. He bought the old brine baths in 1882 and modernised and reopened them six years later as St Andrew's Brine Baths. In such ways he really began to turn what had been a dirty industrial town into an attractive spa.

Other benefactions included donations to educational institutions, including schools and colleges, and not least the building of the row of twelve almshouses by the main road at Wychbold with a stone plaque inscribed: 'THESE ALMSHOUSES WERE ERECTED IN THE YEAR 1895 BY JOHN CORBETT OF IMPNEY, LATE PROPRIETOR OF STOKE PRIOR SALT WORKS AND M.P. FOR DROITWICH AND MID. WORCESTERSHIRE, FOR DECAYED SALT MAKERS, OR THEIR WIDOWS, OF THE COUNTY OF WORCESTER.'

The Chateau Impney and Corbett's marriage breakdown

Much of Corbett's wealth in later years came not from his salt works which, in the face of increasing competition, produced little profit in the late 1870s and the 1880s, but from his extensive investments in land and property and in businesses, including railways and canals. Remaining Corbett estates eventually auctioned in 1920 extended to 1,686 acres including ten large farms and many smallholdings, cottages and other premises. One outstanding purchase by Corbett from the Somers family around 1868 was the Impney Manor Estate of some 200 acres near Droitwich. In 1872 he and his family moved from Stoke Grange into Impney Lodge on the estate, and this was their address until the Chateau Impney, built to replace the old manor house, was ready for occupation. They did, however, live for some time at Perdiswell House, Worcester, until about 1877 when they took up residence at the Chateau. The imposing French chateau-style mansion was planned and designed to rival the Packingtons' Westwood Park and to please Anna Eliza. It took many years to build, as reported in *Kelly's Worcestershire Directory* of 1884: 'Impney, the seat of John Corbett esq., M.P., D.L., J.P., was completed in

John and Anna Eliza Corbett in their early years and in their later years.

1880, after being eleven years in construction.' Unfortunately, by the time the Corbetts moved into their new palatial home, a rift between John and his wife and children had developed. A sixth child, Clare, had been born in 1876 at Perdiswell House, and it has been alleged that John suspected that the father was the priest at Hadzor Roman Catholic Church which was close to the Impney Estate and where Anna was a regular worshipper. Whether or not this was the final straw leading to the breakup of their marriage, the religious difference, the age difference and the difference in temperament between John and Anna must have largely contributed to it. In 1884, by a deed of separation, they parted company, she taking with her their four daughters to live in Somerset. Although Corbett continued to live at the Chateau (known initially as Impney Hall) until his death, he knew no married happiness there and must have been a sadly disillusioned man, especially since in earlier years he had extolled the blessings of married life in messages to his workpeople.

Earlier, in 1878, Corbett had decided to buy a mansion at Towyn on the Welsh Coast called Ynys-y-Maengwen. At first the Corbetts used to spend some time there as a family, but in the months before their separation Anna and the daughters were banished there. Afterwards Corbett himself used the property and he took an interest in the local community, contributing generously to the development of the esplanade, the town's water supply and sewage system, and a school.

Works management and performance

As Corbett's outside interests and travels took up more and more of his time, his workpeople saw less and less of him and the management and smooth running of his works were left in the hands of his general manager, his chief engineer, managers of departments and foremen. Around 1860 the manager of the works was Mr R J Watt, the mechanical engineer was Matthew Bohill, accountant G H Hornsby, and the cashier, as already mentioned, T B O'Meara. In the 1870s and 1880s the general manager was John Brydone, whose residence was Field View, Stoke Heath, and who was also a manager of Stoke Works School. John Gardner of Meadowbank, engineer to the works in the latter part of the Corbett era, was reputed to be a brilliant engineer and to have enlarged the former Imperial works' south pit to a diameter of six feet. Other officials at this time included accountant George S Dee, clerks William Mosson and John Jones, and foremen George Eachus and George Fryer.

When John Corbett took over the BAC works in 1852, production of salt was about 26,000 tons per year. After leasing the ex-Imperial works in 1858, the annual output must have doubled to over 50,000 tons. By 1880, according to Corbett himself, his works was capable of producing 200,000 tons per annum but, due to competition and over-production in the salt industry, output in the 1870s, with some pans unused, was limited to around 150,000 tons per annum. When, in 1889, Corbett sold out to the Salt Union, Stoke Works was producing around 170,000 tons of salt a year. These figures are some measure of the success of Corbett in developing what he himself was proud to call the 'Model

Salt Works of Europe'. In so doing he was able to make for himself a large personal fortune, which was augmented by the income from the ownership of land and farms in which he invested widely.

Events leading to the Salt Union takeover

The 1870s and 1880s were difficult times for the salt industry. Due to increasing competition at home and cheap imports, prices remained low. Parts of many salt works remained idle, and there was little profit to be made. Corbett was faced with local competiton from the neighbouring Droitwich Salt Co, and in the early 1870s there was bitter acrimony between him and the Droitwich manager, John Bradley, over price-cutting. They were on better terms towards the end of the decade when Bradley was more cooperative. From the surviving volume of copies of Corbett's business letters for the years 1870-78, we learn that he corresponded with leading salt makers in Cheshire during that period and met with them, trying to negotiate sensible prices. His approach to his business rivals was, though firm, always courteous and conciliatory. He attended, when he could, the monthly meetings held in Northwich or Crewe of the Salt Chamber of Commerce, which had been founded in 1858 primarily to promote the interests of the salt trade in government legislation, and he was on friendly terms with its official, John Moore. There was evidently a growing realisation amongst the salt producers of the need for mutual understanding and unanimity, which led to mergers in Cheshire, moves to amalgamate, and eventually to the creation of the Salt Union.

The 1880s saw the upsurge of the trade union movement and agitation amongst the labouring classes for increased wages. No doubt many of John Corbett's employees contrasted their own wages and conditions in smoky Stoke with the affluence and palatial home of their master at Impney, not realising that his wealth was now not from salt but from his property and investments. For some years a Saltmakers' Society had been in existence in Cheshire, a welfare rather than a trades organisation, and a similar society came into being in Droitwich. In July 1889, on the recommendation of Mr Broadhurst MP, the societies of salt makers at Droitwich and Stoke, consisting of 200 members, agreed at a meeting in Droitwich to amalgamate with the Cheshire District Salt Makers Association with 1200 members at Winsford and 600 at Northwich, to become one body, the Salt Makers Union, with its headquarters at Winsford.

The formation of the the Salt Union, which brought together the greater part of the British salt industry, was largely due to the initiative of Herman E Falk, salt proprietor of Winsford and merchant in Liverpool. His first scheme in 1884 for the amalgamation of the major salt producers was rejected; but a second attempt in 1887 was favourably received, because by then cut-throat competition between the producers had brought the industry to unprofitable chaos. There was also the need to present a united front in the face of the growing threat of united action on the part of disgruntled salt workers. The

Salt Union was registered on 6 October 1888, following a meeting in Liverpool the previous July when conditions and terms were agreed, and it was authorised to raise £3 million in £10 shares plus £1 million in debentures. It was heavily over-subscribed to the extent of £35 million. Sixty-five vendors, including John Corbett, sold their salt works to the new company, representing 85 per cent of all UK salt production. The first board of directors comprised six London businessmen, not hitherto connected with the salt business, together with seven salt industrialists, including John Corbett who was appointed vice-chairman of the board. He held 10,000 shares in the company, besides debentures, worth altogether £125,000.

The £3.7 million which the Salt Union paid for all the properties it took over included £600,000 to John Corbett for his Stoke Prior Works. These had been valued at £400,000, but Corbett, during negotiations in the early months of 1888, had shown himself reluctant to relinquish the ownership of his works, and the promotors of the Salt Union, to persuade him to do so and to net this vital fish, had no alternative but to pay the inflated price. Stoke Works was conveyed to the Salt Union under the terms of an agreement dated 24 January and a deed of covenant dated 5 March 1889. At the outset, Corbett was appointed managing director of the Worcestershire Division, which included Stoke Works and the Droitwich Salt Works, at a salary of £1,000 per annum; so, though no longer the owner of Stoke Works, he still exercised at first considerable control over it. But things were soon to change.

Postcard of Stoke Works showing the fountain (ornamental miniature water tower) erected by John Corbett in 1882 for the villagers. It was demolished in 1928 when no longer needed.

Chapter 3

Under the Salt Union and ICI: 1889-1972

John Corbett and the Salt Union, 1889-94

The first few years of the Salt Union were rather turbulent. Disputes soon arose between individual 'salt directors', still involved in salt production, and the 'London directors', financiers, over pricing and administrative policies, over the interpretation of the written agreements made when the various salt works were purchased, and over the use of former trademarks. Stoke Works was no exception. Friction between John Corbett and the Salt Union over these issues soon developed and led him to resign his positions as a director of the Salt Union in 1891 and as managing director of the Worcestershire Division early in 1892. In February 1892 he issued a circular to the Salt Union shareholders prior to their third annual general meeting which, due to ill health, he was unable to attend. In it he complained: 'Some of the clauses in my deed of covenant have been repeatedly and persistently infringed to the loss of many thousands to the shareholders.' He also complained about 'the overt opposition to my authority and management, as compared with other works purchased by the Salt Union'. Whereas the average overall profit of the Salt Union in the three years 1889-91 was 7 per cent per annum of its total investment, Corbett pointed out that the profits of Stoke Works alone in this period amounted to over £200,000, an average of over 11 per cent per annum of the Salt Union's investment of £600,000 in the works. He also claimed that the high price of salt fixed by the Salt Union had depressed the trade and caused part of his works to stand idle. His advice that prices should be lowered was, in fact, subsequently taken. The continuing dispute and litigation came to a head in 1894 when an agreement, without trial, was reached under which the 'Salt King' allowed himself to be banished from his industrial realm, the Stoke Prior and the Droitwich works, and accepted legal restraints upon his future business activities, in return for a generous financial settlement.

When the Salt Union acquired Corbett's works in 1889 it did not at the same time purchase his warehouses, wharves and agencies in London, Birmingham, Gloucester and elsewhere, nor his fleet of boats, nor the trade names under which he had sold his various brands of salt. So he retained his distribution business and facilities, and continued as an independent salt merchant. This was a source of irritation to the Salt Union and a loophole in its trading and pricing controls. By 1894 John Corbett, having suffered several bouts of ill health and perhaps weary of the hassle, was ready to dispose of his distribution and sales business, and glad to retire from the salt trade, which had brought him wealth and fame, in order to devote more time to his other interests.

Under the agreement dated 10 April 1894 and effective from the following 1 July, Corbett sold his business as a distributor of salt to the Salt Union for £60,000. The transfer included the whole of his home and export trade and agencies and all trademarks for thirty years, and he was restricted from carrying on any business directly or indirectly in connection with the manufacture or sale of salt. For the next thirty years Corbett's baths at Droitwich were to be supplied by the Salt Union free of charge with all the brine required for working them. Messrs Weston and Fox were to be retained as London agents of the Salt Union for seven years, each at a salary of £1,200 a year. All Corbett's leases of warehouses, wharves and offices in London, Gloucester and elsewhere were assigned to the Salt Union, together with all stocks, horses, vans, plant and materials. The Salt Union undertook to retain the services of the whole of Corbett's staff of clerks and travellers at Stoke Prior for at least three years, subject to good behaviour. The previous agreement and deed of covenant of 1889 between Corbett and the Salt Union were cancelled. So the Salt Union was now in complete control of the works and, from it, the distribution and sale of salt at home and overseas; but Corbett had made sure that the jobs of many of his key workers were safeguarded for some time at least.

In the event, the London agency, Weston and Westall of 115 Lower Thames Street, which Corbett had inherited from the BAC and which was managed by Weston and Fox, immediately formed a limited company with a nominal capital of £20,000 and bought their business back from the Salt Union for £11,432 on 2 July 1894. They were able to rent the London depots, whose leases the Salt Union had just acquired from Corbett. It evidently suited the Salt Union to retain an independently managed and well-established sales organisation in the London area.

William Young's management, 1894-1910

Following Corbett's retirement from the management of the Stoke and Droitwich Works of the Salt Union at the end of June 1894, the new manager appointed by the Salt Union was William Young. A letter book of carbon copies of his official letters from August 1894 to February 1900 (in the St Helen's branch of the Worcester Record Office) reveals that, apart from the actual management of the Stoke and Droitwich Works, a number of issues engaged his attention, and many of his letters were to inform the then chairman of the Salt Union, the Hon Lionel Ashley, and its general manager, J M Fells Esq, of these issues and developments.

In Droitwich in the early 1890s there were four independent salt producers outside the Salt Union, and William Young spent considerable time and effort in assessing their viability and in trying to negotiate their takeover, or at least to minimise their competitiveness. The small firm of Causier, which was barely profitable, was soon bought out; likewise the former Fardon's works and Dunster's works (which the Salt Union in 1888 had refused to buy), both owned by John Bradley. But efforts to take over the works of J P Harvey & Co and of Boucher and Giles met with resistance and legal complications over lost deeds, brine rights, and the ownership of wayleaves for brine pipes under some streets of the town. At great legal expense the Salt Union, which had acquired Droitwich territorial brine rights from Corbett, was able in 1897 to obtain an injunction against the use by J P Harvey & Co of brine pipes which they had laid under some Droitwich streets, as well as an order for their removal; this despite opposition from the borough of Droitwich. So J P Harvey & Co were put out of business. Boucher and Giles, however, managed to survive until around 1918.

Another problem arose over the brine baths in Droitwich which were extended and required 50 per cent more brine than was needed when the 1894 agreement with John Corbett had been made for their free supply. In 1895 a legal settlement in favour of the Salt Union stipulated that only the original amount should continue to be supplied free of charge. There were also, for a time, other minor disputes with Corbett over unpaid bills and other items.

Launched with high hopes of financial success, the Salt Union soon found itself struggling. To induce the proprietors to part with their salt works, it had paid grossly high prices, in some cases, as for Stoke Works, 50 per cent above their valuation; so it began by raising salt prices. The price of fine salt, for instance, which was 24 shillings per ton in October 1888, had risen to 48 shillings by February 1889. The resulting high profit margins encouraged the smaller producers outside the Salt Union to expand and undercut it, and also led to some new firms setting up in business. This competition was a serious threat and, together with diminishing overseas sales as other countries began to produce more of their own salt, caused the union's output of salt to drop from 1.6 million tons in 1889 to less than 1 million tons by 1898. Dividends on ordinary shares in the company fell from 7 per cent in 1889 to 3 per cent in 1894; and from 1897 to 1914 ordinary shareholders received no interest apart from 1¼ per cent in 1907. The price of ordinary £10 shares dropped from £11 10s to £1 10s in the first ten years. One significant factor in the decline in the fortunes of the Salt Union at this time was the replacement in the chemical industry of the Leblanc process for producing alkali from solid salt, in use for about a century, by the Solvay (ammonia-soda) process which uses brine. As a result, the union's sales of salt for chemicals fell from 600,000 tons per annum in 1891 to around 100,000 tons by 1905.

In 1905 the parent company, Salt Union Limited, appointed G W Malcolm as its chief engineer. A man who realised the need for the rationalisation and modernisation of the company's plants, he was appointed its managing director in 1913. In that same year F W Clark became sales manager and associate managing director. Under the wise and efficient management of these two men the fortunes of the Salt Union began to recover and from 1915 onwards it was able to pay modest dividends. Output of salt had risen to around 450,000 tons by 1936, shortly before the ICI takeover.

Harry Lockhead's management, 1910-30

In October 1910 Henry (Harry) Lockhead from Winsford succeeded William Young as manager of the Salt Union's Droitwich and Stoke Works, and he remained in office until his death in 1930. During his twenty years of management the open-pan method of salt production continued with few major changes.

In Worcestershire, under the Salt Union, there had been very little interruption of output due to strike action, but from June to August 1914 there was a general eight-week long strike of salt makers which came to an end with the outbreak of the 1914-18 War. During the war production was maintained by the older men not called up; women were still excluded from all but the two packaging departments in the old mill on the east side and the new mill on the west side of the canal.

One major development during Harry Lockhead's regime was the introduction of electricity to the Stoke Works. This occurred immediately following World War One. A coal-fired power station was built to the left of the main gates, near to the tall chimney. This generated direct current and supplied the whole works with electric light and power. The generators were steam-powered from large coal-fired boilers, the smoke from which went up the tall Gossage chimney. The steam engines which had been used up to that time for driving machinery in various parts of the works were soon replaced by electric motors. It was at this time, in 1920, that the brine pumps began to be worked by electricity instead of by steam power.

Surface mechanism for the pumps of numbers 1 and 2 brine pits, showing the wooden superstructure above each pit.

A major change in working conditions at Stoke was introduced in 1921 with the replacement of the two-shift system, started by John Corbett in 1859, by a working day of three shifts. The two twelve-hour shifts had been from 6 am to 6 pm and 6 pm to 6 am and men had worked alternate weeks on day and night shifts. The three shifts were mainly from 6 am to 2 pm, 2 pm to 10 pm and 10

Chapter 3

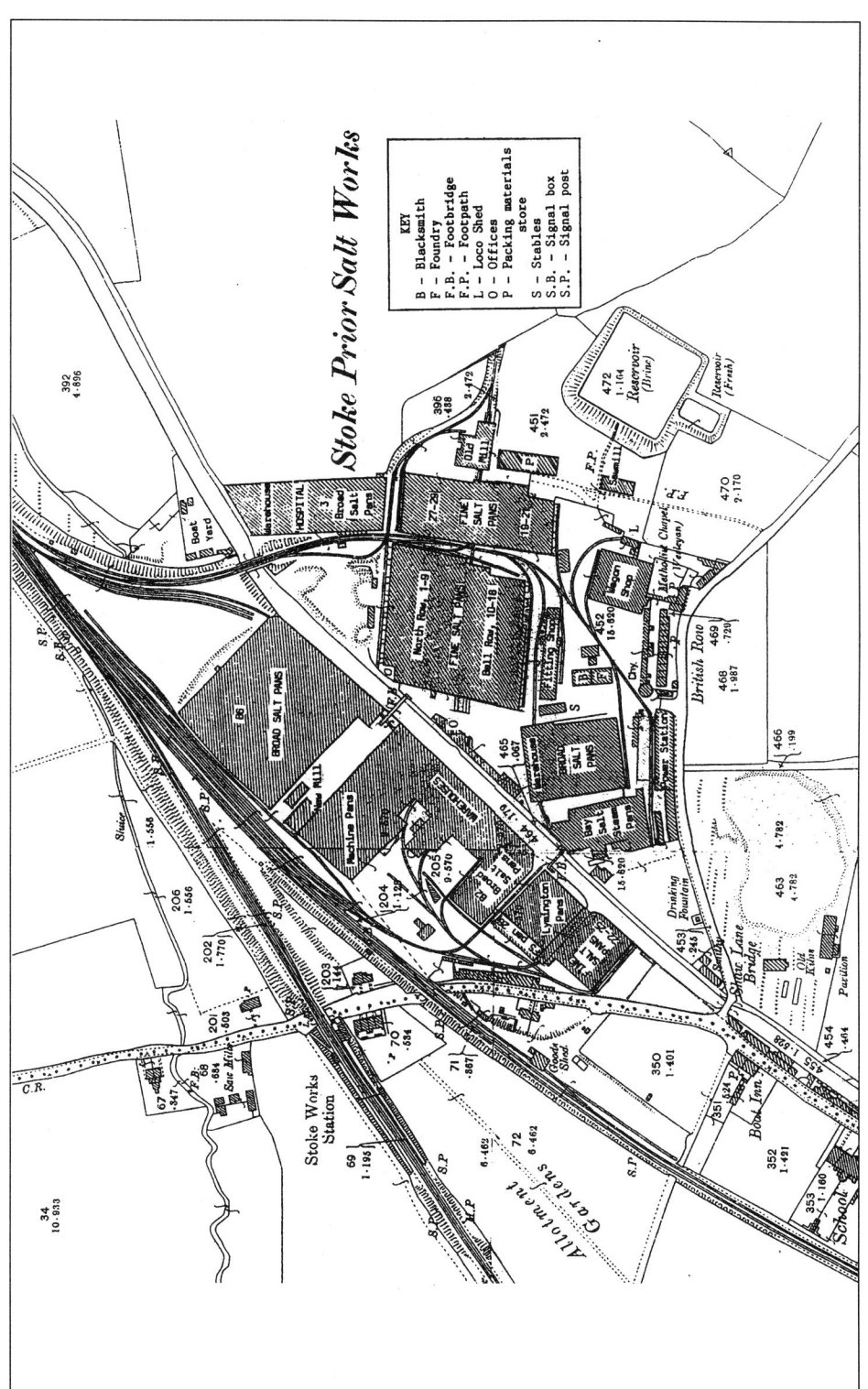

Stoke Prior Salt Works under the Salt Union, early 1920s.

pm to 6 am. These changes were in line with general postwar improvements in working conditions in industry.

In 1922 the Salt Union closed down its Droitwich Covercroft Works in pursuit of its programme of rationalisation, which involved the elimination of its smaller less efficient plants. Most of the Droitwich employees and some of the plant were transferred to Stoke Works, and a special train was put on by the LMS Railway Company to get the workers from Droitwich to Stoke Works Station by 7.15 am. With these extra workers the workforce at Stoke Works rose to around 550. By the 1930s Stoke Works was one of only seven of the larger works which remained out of the sixty-five salt works originally purchased by the Salt Union.

By the people of Stoke Works Harry Lockhead was chiefly remembered for the large part he played in bringing into being the Stoke Works Recreation Club on the site of the old Corbett brickworks. In 1922 he wrote to the Stoke Prior Cricket Club (which had been in existence since 1860) for their assistance; and they agreed to become the first section of the new club on condition that villagers who were not employed at the salt works could also become members. This was agreed, and there followed some years of work, mostly by volunteers, to clear the derelict site on which, during the war, there had been a sawmill. Three tennis courts, two bowling greens, pavilions, and pitches for cricket and football were created, and these were in use by 1924-5. A club building which included a tearoom and an assembly hall for dances, concerts and other events was completed and opened in January 1929. On 6 July of that year Mr Malcolm, managing director of the Salt Union, and his wife were amongst seventy guests from the Winsford and London staffs of the Salt Union who sat down with forty of the Stoke Works staff to a lunch in the new assembly hall, when Mr Lockhead was congratulated on all he had done to provide for the social needs of the people of Stoke Works. Reference was also made on that occasion to the new salt works offices being built nearby by Messrs J & A Brazier of Bromsgrove. The new office block, on the opposite side of the Hanbury Road to the old BAC works' entrance, was opened in December 1929 and provided much better facilities than the old offices above the canal arm.

Later works managers

Following the death of Harry Lockhead in 1930, the works manager for the next seven years was Mr S T T Geary, a Cambridge mathematician, a brilliant chemist and a historian and statistician of railway locomotives. He was in charge when, in 1937, Stoke Works became part of the Salt Division of ICI. Imperial Chemical Industries Ltd had been formed in 1926 by a merger of the major Cheshire alkali company, Brunner and Mond, with other large chemical companies. In 1937 ICI purchased all the Salt Union's interests, and thus Stoke Works became a part of ICI's business empire. An early consequence of the takeover was the appointment of Alex Miscampbell (known as Paddy) from the former Salt Union's Carrickfergus works in Northern Ireland to succeed

A fine-salt pan with a row of filled tubs inside it draining partially before being removed and stacked against the wall to drain further for the salt to solidify.

Inside a fine-salt panhouse stove, showing new squares on a trolley being moved to a catpath alongside other squares drying on the flat top of a flue, and showing squares stacked high above the return flue.

Mr Geary as general manager at Stoke. Miscampbell departed in 1940 and was succeeded by his deputy, Harry Ward, who continued to manage the open-pan salt production until it finished in 1956.

Salt production under the Salt Union

When the ICI took over, the Salt Union's works comprised three pits and pumphouses, twenty-nine fine-salt open pans, four patent covered machine pans, fourteen broad-salt pans, two salt mills and packing departments, and all the various ancillary works including a foundry, wagon shop, fitting shop, timber yard, sawmill and offices. The plant was still basically the same as it had been at the end of the Corbett era, except that the number of broad-salt pans in use had been reduced by about 50 per cent due to a decline in the demand for crystal salt in industry, and the number of round machine pans had been gradually reduced from sixteen (seven for squares, nine for butter salt) to four (for squares), as explained below. Drastic changes were on the way under ICI but, following the outbreak of the 1939-45 War, these had to wait.

Under the open-pan system of salt production, still in operation when ICI took over, various grades of salt were manufactured at Stoke. Fine-salt pans, 21-25 feet wide, 30-40 feet long, and 18-20 inches deep, produced table salt (the brine boiled at the maximum temperature of 226°F), and fine common salt (the brine evaporated at 220°F). As it formed, the fine salt was raked to the side of the pan and ladled, using perforated concave shovels called 'skimmers', into wooden tubs made of wet elm. These square-sectioned tubs with small drain holes tapered slightly towards the bottom and were of various sizes to produce large blocks of salt described as 160s (i.e. 160 to the ton, each 14 lb weight), 120s (each about 19 lb), 112s (20 lb), and 80s (28 lb). 160s were about 8 inches square and 2 feet long; others were proportionally larger. Each tub was put into the side of the pan to be filled, until there was a row of filled tubs within the pan on that side. They were then lifted out and left to drain by the wall of the pan room.

The salt maker filled 60 to 90 tubs on one side of the pan then transferred to the other side, by which time the blocks of salt in the tubs previously filled were solid enough for the tubs to be upturned and the blocks of salt deposited onto the level platform of a long trolley wagon. Two narrow 15-inch gauge tramways, one each side, ran the length of the panhouse and a trolley wagon on each facilitated the movement of the salt blocks (called 'squares'), fourteen to sixteen at a time, from the panroom into the stove (drying room) where they were placed on a low shelf of hard salt called a 'catpath'. From the three furnaces situated under each pan there ran two metal flues about 4 feet wide and 4 feet high, raised above the level of the floor and extending to the far end of the stove where they came together into one central return flue under the floor to the chimney, which rose through the stove beside the wall separating the panroom from the stove. There was a catpath on each side of the raised flues, and each tramroad from the panroom was divided by a set of points to run along each side of the corresponding raised flue so that squares could be

Chapter 3

The sawmill where squares were sawn into cut lumps. When work was in progress there was a cloud of salt dust, which in later times was largely prevented with extractor ducts.

Female salt packers at work wrapping cut lumps, c.1910.

conveyed to either of its catpaths. After a day drying on the catpaths, the squares were moved by a lofter onto the top of the flues to dry out further for another day. They were then moved by the lofter into a stack in the centre of the stove above the return flue. It was the job of loaders to move the squares, using barrows, and load them into wagons or canal boats, or take them to one of the mills to be processed.

The fine-salt maker worked an eight-hour shift on his own. It was literally sweated labour, stripped to the waist in the hot steam-filled panroom. He had to stoke his own furnaces, keep his salt pan raked to prevent the pan burning, fill about 300 tubs each shift, and move the squares by trolley to the catpaths in the stove. Fine-salt pans were worked continuously in eight-hour shifts, twenty-four hours a day, from early Monday morning, when the furnaces were cleaned out and lit and the first shift got the pan of brine to boiling point, to Saturday mid-day, when the furnaces were let out. The lofters, one to each fine-salt panhouse, worked the usual 7.30 am to 5.00 pm daytime stint (7.30 am to 1.00 pm on Saturdays), and on weekdays moved about 900 squares from flue to stack and 900 from catpath to flue. A team of loaders also worked the daytime stint and went round from panhouse to panhouse, taking away the salt.

The 160s, 120s and 80s lumps were dispatched, either wrapped or unwrapped, for sale to food manufacturers, in shops, or by street vendors who would cut up the lumps to sell to their customers. The 112s, known as 'top-hats', went to one of the two mills to be sawn up into 2 lb or 1 lb blocks (known as 'cut lumps') which were wrapped by women ready for dispatch in cartons or in wooden boxes for export. Some thirty women were engaged in this work. They were paid 4d per gross (144) of lumps wrapped, and they could wrap 20 to 25 gross of cut lumps in a day. The salt often made their fingers so sore that they had to be bound up. In the mill the offcuts from sawing the top-hats to make cut lumps, together with broken lumps, were ground to produce dairy salt. This was packed into bags of various sizes ranging from 7 lb to 1 cwt.

A limited amount of fine salt called Lymington Salt was made in three fine-salt pans in a building on the west side of the canal. It was not put into tubs and made into squares but was dried loose and bagged.

During the making of fine salt the boiling caused a layer of hard salt, called panscale, to form on the bottom of the pan. This layer could be several inches thick, and every few days, two or three times a fortnight, the furnaces were damped down, the pan was emptied and the panscale chipped off using picks and crowbars. This process was known as 'scabbing up', and the hard lumps obtained by it were called 'picking'. Scabbing up was usually done by the fine-salt maker on an afternoon shift. It took an hour or so to do; then it took the rest of the shift time to stoke up the furnaces and get the newly-filled pan of brine boiling. Some picking was sold to farmers for cattle lick. Large lumps, heated in the domestic oven and wrapped in flannel, were used by many salt workers and their families as bedwarmers, though if left in the bed they could cause bruises. Picking was also ground in the picking mill and sold for chemical and agricultural use.

Broad salt of various types was produced in large pans around 125 feet long

Chapter 3

Broad-salt pans at Stoke Works, showing brine pipes.

Broad salt being shovelled out and heaped on elm hurdles to drain.

Inside a fine-salt panhouse stove. Loaders removing squares from the stack.

Inside a broad-salt warehouse. Salt being put into 2-cwt sacks for export.

and 25 feet wide. These were heated either by three or four furnaces under the width of the pan or by steam. Common salt, consisting of crystals about the size of granulated sugar, was formed by evaporation of brine at 180°F and took two days to produce. To produce fishery salt, with crystals about ¼ inch in size, evaporation was at 140°F and took three to four days. Very large crystalline salt called bay salt, with crystals 1 to 2 inches in size, took up to four weeks to form at a temperature of 120°F. Crystalisation of bay salt was assisted by the presence of twigs or wrapping twine in the pan, which was heated by steam from the works powerhouse. Workers on the broad-salt pans were known as broad-salt drawers. Other men, furnacemen and loaders were also involved. Most just worked the usual daytime hours, 7.30 am to 5.00 pm.

As already mentioned, there were sixteen round patent machine pans in operation when the Salt Union took over John Corbett's works, each producing very fine high density salt. They were housed in a building on the west side of, and away from, the canal. The salt from seven of these pans was put into tubs to make squares which were dried in a nearby large stove. Salt from the other nine pans was dried loose in a warehouse, bagged and sold as 'butter salt'. Steam from the patent pans was used to heat nearby broad-salt pans. The broad salt thus produced was dried and stored in a large warehouse alongside the canal.

Close to the patent machine salt panroom was the new mill where cut lumps were sawn and wrapped and where there was a cube plant with machinery to cut so-called 'salt cubes' which were 1 inch square by $7/16$ inch thick and were each the equivalent of a tablespoonful of salt. The cubes, cut from patent-salt squares, were put by women salt packers into packets and sold as 'Falk's Salt Cubes'.

Under the Salt Union the production of butter salt from the machine pans gradually declined and it ceased at the end of 1917. By the time of the ICI takeover only four patent pans remained in use, producing squares. In spite of the greater efficiency of the machine pans their repair and replacement was much more costly than than that of conventional open pans. It seems that as they wore out they were not renewed or replaced.

World War Two and the end of salt carrying by canal

During the 1939-45 War salt production was maintained, salt being a vital commodity, and few salt workers were called up to serve in the forces. In an air raid at 2.10 am (British Double Summer Time) on 10 May 1941 two German bombs were dropped. One inside the works failed to explode. The other hit the railway line at the back of the house of the Stoke Works station master, William Salcombe. It blew a wooden sleeper through the window of a nearby house and an 80-foot rail into his garden. It also damaged a large area of the roof of the broad-salt pans nearby, scattering slates over a wide area, but salt production was not affected.

Earlier in 1941 there was an air raid over Birmingham and a bomb destroyed the salt warehouse of Henry Johnson Ltd, the Salt Union's agents, of

Patent covered machine pans introduced by John Corbett.

Another view showing tubs filled from the trough of a machine pan and squares on a trolley for moving to the stove (drying room).

Holt Street, Gosta Green. That night the last salt-carrying boat *Joan*, owned by Johnson's, was moored outside the warehouse and was damaged beyond repair. Fortunately the crew, Jack Merrell and his mate Jack Mayo, had slipped home for the night. But that was the end of the canal carrying of salt from Stoke Works. This means of transport had been at its peak during the Corbett era. When John Corbett sold his works to the Salt Union in 1889, his fleet of boats was not included, and several more boats were registered in his name in 1890 and 1891. Nor were his boats involved in the agreement by which, on 1 July 1894, he sold his distribution business, agencies, depots, wharves and trademarks to the Salt Union. However, a separate agreement was negotiated in October of 1894 under which the Salt Union paid Corbett £3,765 14s, the agreed value of his boats, fixures, fittings, bags and stock-in-trade.

The number of Corbett boats re-registered by the Salt Union in Birmingham in 1895 was only fourteen. Others may have been registered in Worcester; but the Salt Union, it seems, acquired less than half of Corbett's fleet of boats, the remainder being either scrapped or sold to others, including George Farrin, who became an independent boat-builder and boat-owner, and Henry Johnson Ltd. By 1914 the Salt Union owned only eight boats, including *Medway* and *Cynthia*, worked by Dennis Merrell, *Albion* and *Progress* by Albert Coleman, *Thistle* by James Wright, *Victory* by John Wright and *Ripple* by Billy Brown. In the early 1920s just six boats were operated under the Salt Union, amongst them *Medway*, now manned by Dennis Merrell's sons Jack and Denny, and *Victory* by Jack Wright and Harry Bourne. By 1927 these two

Salt cubes being produced by machinery and packed in the new mill on the west side of the canal.

were the only remaining salt boats, and after 1927 only *Medway* survived, being replaced in 1938 by a new boat, *Joan*, built by Nursers of Braunston. During the earlier years of the Salt Union's management of Stoke Works a great deal of salt was shipped down to Gloucester by general carriers including the Severn and Canal Carrying Company and Jacob Rice and Sons of Gloucester, and by individual boat-owners such as William Giddins, William Russell and 'Filly' Franklin.

The ICI vacuum plant

Following the end of the Second World War in 1945, ICI proceeded with plans and preparations for the building of a vacuum plant at Stoke Works. Many of the old saltworks buildings on the west side of the canal were demolished, and the building of the vacuum plant began on 16 October 1946, supervised by Jock Kerr. As it neared completion in 1949, Winston May, a chemist from Cheshire, was appointed plant manager. The plant opened on 30 June 1950 and May remained to develop and monitor it for many years, succeeded by Frank Harding who remained until it closed.

The first Salt Union vacuum plant had been erected at Winsford, Cheshire, way back in 1905. This was followed in 1911 by the erection of a much larger and more efficient plant at Weston Point, near Runcorn, Cheshire, the brine for which was pumped along an eleven-mile pipe line from Marston, near Northwich. At Weston Point, as was the case later at Stoke, high-pressure steam was passed through turbines on its way from the boiler to produce cheap electricity. Much more electricity was produced than was needed in the vacuum plant, so the Salt Union formed a subsidiary, the Mersey Power Company Limited, to distribute and sell this surplus electricity, and this proved to be a profitable sideline.

At Stoke Works the new vacuum plant comprised several buildings. The largest one, a long tall building facing the canal, had two parts. In the larger northern end were the brine evaporators and ancillary equipment for producing and processing the salt. In the southern end was the dried-salt warehouse and packaging plant. Behind the main building and separated from it by a roadway was the undried-salt warehouse connected to the main building by a high walkway with two salt conveyers. Beyond this was the lofty boilerhouse with its tall chimney and lean-to powerhouse. A great coal bunker high above the boilerhouse was filled by means of a wagon-tipper and bucket-elevator. From the bunker coal was fed by a chute into a large Babcock and Wilcock boiler which burnt about 130 tons of coal per week and raised steam at a pressure of 600 lb per square inch. The high-pressure steam was first used to power a turbine in the powerhouse which drove the generator to produce electricity for the works. The exhaust steam from the turbine then passed to the salt-producing plant in the main building.

The vacuum-plant building had four access levels with metal lattice flooring between the ground and top floors. On the concrete ground floor were various tanks and pumps. The first floor gave access to the undersides of the five

Farrin's dockyard in 1906, showing boats under construction, a new motorboat built for T & M Dixon of Tardebigge, and (right) a Worcester Porcelain Company's boat which carried broad salt for use in the glazing of porcelain. This was John Corbett's boatyard until 1894.

The last salt boat on the Worcester and Birmingham Canal, Joan, *owned by Henry Johnson Ltd of Holt Street, Birmingham, and skippered by Jack Merrell, is here seen giving children an outing. The boat wa damaged beyond repair in an air raid on Birmingham in 1941.*

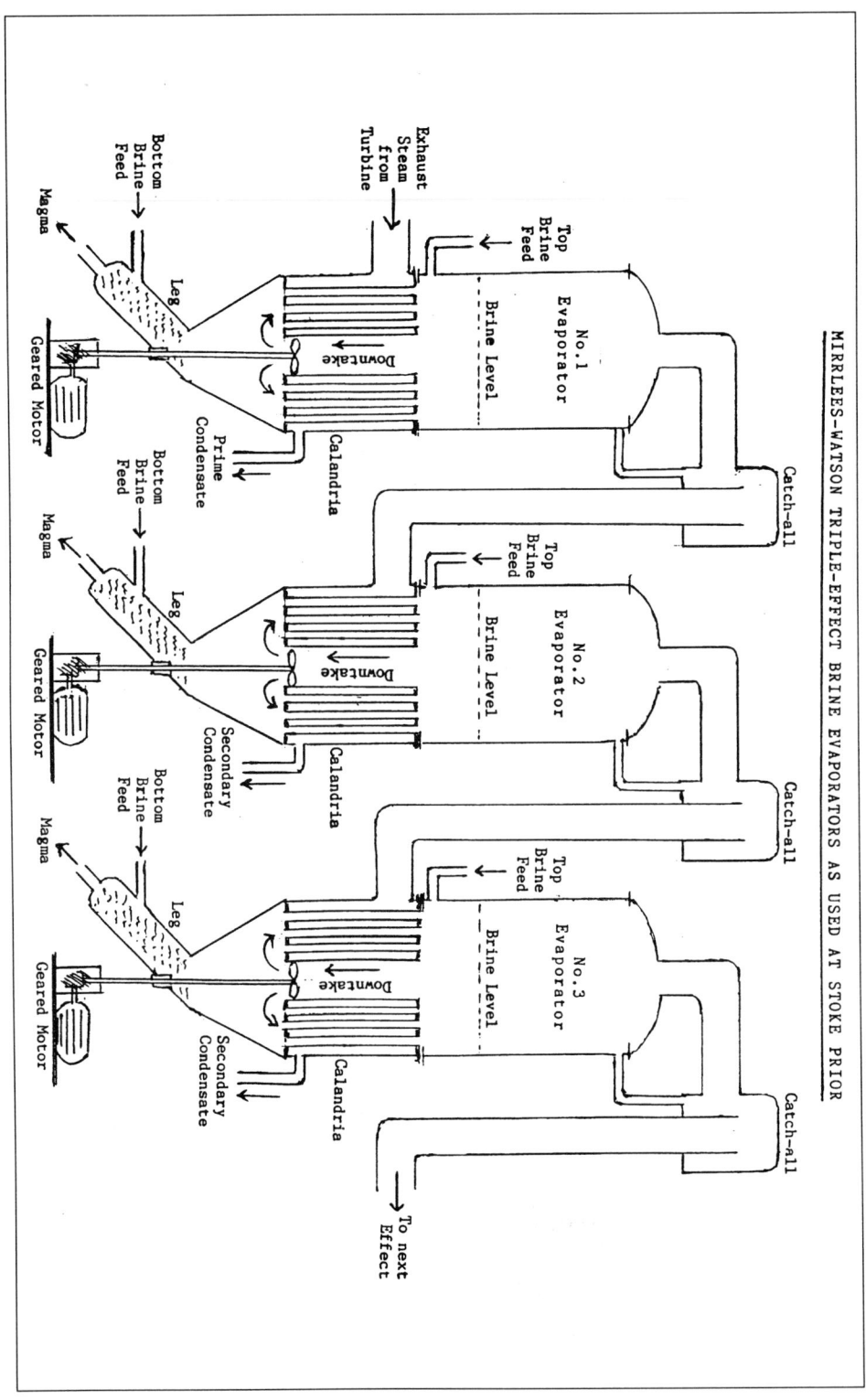

Chapter 3

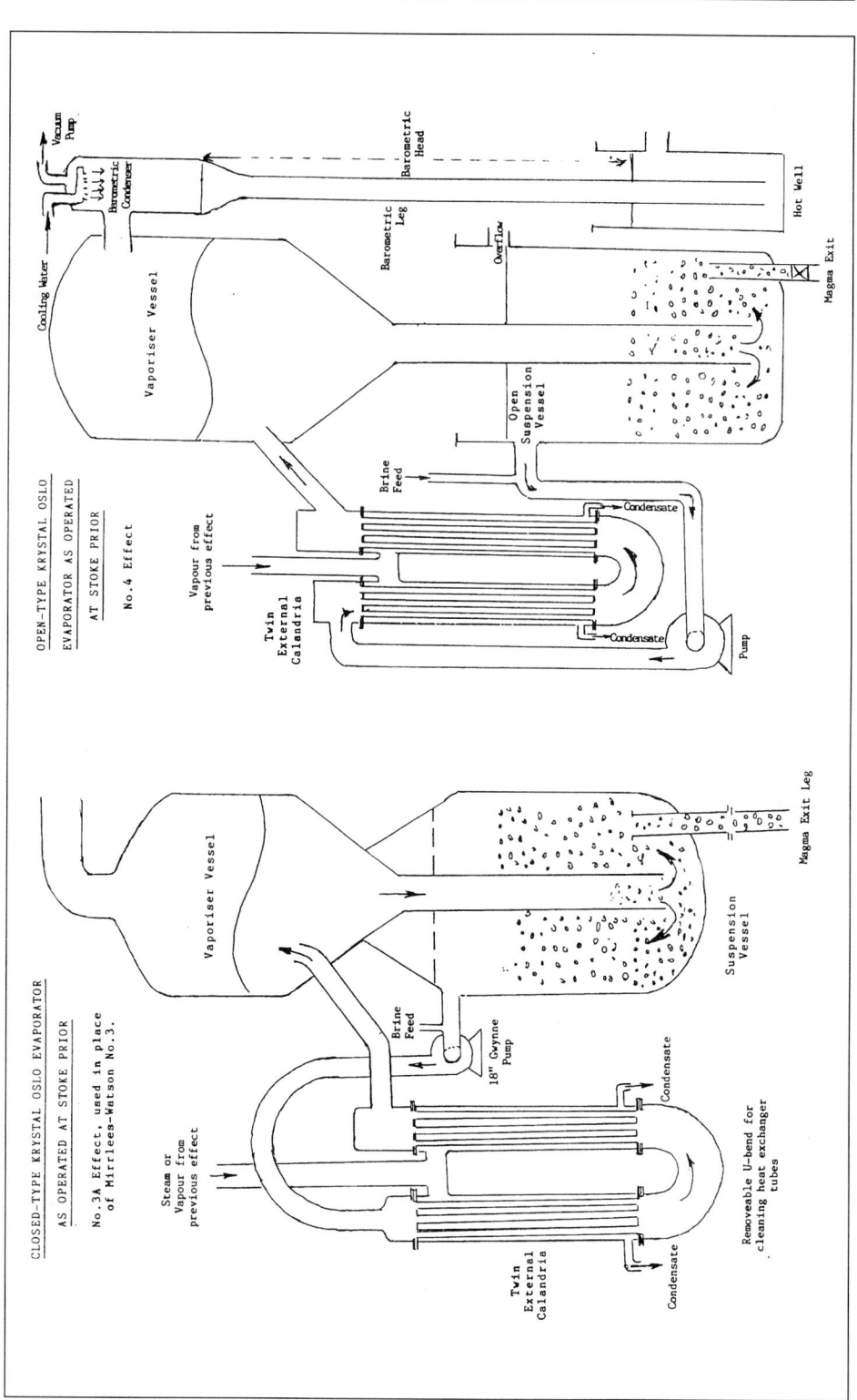

evaporators which mainly occupied the lofty second floor. On the top floor was the filtration plant.

The brine used in the vacuum plant had to be purified. The main impurities were calcium, magnesium and sulphate. The purification plant consisted essentially of a large mixing tank with a mechanical stirrer, surrounded by four spiral-channel brine settlers. In the mixing tank measured quantities of soda ash (sodium carbonate) and either caustic soda (sodium hydroxide) or hydrated lime (calcium hydroxide) were added to the raw brine and mixed with it. The mixture was then piped to the top centre of each of the four large cylindrical settling tanks. Each settling tank had spiral partitioning in the top cylindrical part, so that the mixture flowed slowly along the spiral channel to the outside edge, by which time the impurities of magnesium and calcium were to a great extent removed in low solubility magnesium hydroxide and calcium carbonate which were precipitated and sank, like a thick whitewash, to the conical base. This chemical waste, called brine sludge, was piped into pits in nearby fields alongside the railway sidings and reached, in time, a depth of four feet. The purified brine overflowed into a channel around the outer rim of each brine settler and was run off.

Initially there were three identical evaporator vessels (or 'effects'), numbered 1,2,3, in line. These formed what was known as a Mirrlees Watson Triple-Effect system, producing fine table salt. A fourth effect (no. 4), of different construction and known as an open-type Kristal Oslo evaporator, was soon added; and this produced a coarse granular salt with rounded crystals

The ICI vacuum plant at Stoke Prior, showing, left to right, the lofty coal bunker, the boilerhouse and powerhouse, the broad-salt warehouse, and (alongside the canal) the fine-salt warehouse and the slightly taller vacuum-plant building.

almost the size of rice grains. The Oslo evaporator was the first of its kind to be used in salt production. It was followed in 1952 by the addition of a fifth closed-type Kristal Oslo evaporator, identified as no. 3A, which operated in place of the no. 3 Mirrlees vessel.

Each of the three Mirrlees Watson evaporators consisted of a large vertical cylinder of cast iron, about 12 feet in diameter and 20 feet tall with a conical base and a shallow curved dome at the top. Right across the middle of each was a calandria (steam chamber) in the shape of a 6 feet 6 inches deep cylinder with many 2½-inch diameter copper tubes running vertically between horizontal top and bottom plates of phosphor-bronze, through which the brine in the evaporators could pass, and by which it was effectively heated. To keep the brine circulating upwards through the calandria tubes, a propellor rotating on a vertical spindle powered from below forced the brine to flow downwards through a tube about 2 feet in diameter in the centre of each calandria. Brine, having passed through the purification plant, was supplied to each of the evaporators through an inlet at the base and by one above the calandria.

The exhaust steam from the turbine, at a pressure of about 15 lb per square inch, was piped into the calandria of no.1 evaporator and caused the brine to boil at about atmospheric pressure to produce fine salt which sank to the base and was piped off with a certain amount of brine as a slurry known as 'magma'. The used steam from the calandria was condensed and returned to the boiler. The steam from the boiling brine was passed through a large pipe from the top of the evaporator into the calandria of no. 2 evaporator vessel to heat its brine under partial vacuum, and in turn the steam from the boiling brine in no. 2 was piped to the calandria of no. 3 or the double calandria of no. 3A effect. Condensation of the steam from the boiling brine in each evaporator helped to reduce the pressure and cause the brine to boil at a lower temperature than it would do at ordinary atmospheric pressure.

The Kristal Oslo evaporators were larger than the others. They were about 15 feet in diameter and were constructed of rubber-lined mild steel. No. 3A used the steam from the evaporation of brine in no. 2 effect to heat its brine in a pair of external calandrias. A circulation pump caused brine from the large closed lower part of the Oslo evaporator, called the suspension vessel, to travel downwards through the tubes of one cylindrical calandria and then upwards through the tubes of the other and into the top part of the evaporator. In the suspension vessel the salt crystals were retained for some time before being run off, in order to allow them to grow to about 1.5 millimetres in diameter. The crystals were rounded by abrasion as they circulated with the brine.

The older no. 4 Oslo evaporator worked on similar lines to no. 3A, with external calandrias, but the lower suspension vessel was open, which meant that it had to be the last effect in a multiple system. Until the arrival of no. 3A closed Oslo effect, it followed no. 3 Mirrlees effect. With 3A in use it was sometimes used to make fine salt.

At first the steam outlet from the final evaporator of the system was connected through a condenser to a vacuum pump, but this was soon replaced by a more efficient steam ejector to reduce the pressure so that the brine in the last effect boiled at a low temperature, around blood heat. To reduce heat loss, all the evaporators were encased in 3-inch thick lagging, as was much of the pipework. A persistent problem was the progressive blockage of the calandria tubes by crystallising salt and slight deposits of sodium sulphate scale. To counteract this they were washed out with boiling water every other day.

From the evaporators the magma was piped into conical tanks situated on the ground floor, one for fine salt and another for the coarser granular salt. From these tanks the magma was pumped up to head tanks at the top of the building, from which it was fed to the top of the rotary vacuum filters which separated the salt from the saturated brine. Each of the filters, one for the fine and one for the granular salt, consisted of a large cylindrical drum rotating slowly on a horizontal axle. The curved surface, called the 'cloth', was a fine mesh of corrosion-resistant Monel alloy, a very close weave for the fine salt and more open for the granular salt. From the inside of each cylinder air was pumped to suck in the brine, whilst the salt remained on the surface and was removed by a fixed scraper at the side of the drum. The brine was recovered and returned to the evaporators. From its filter all the granular salt went to the 'undried' warehouse. Some fine salt was also conveyed to the 'undried' warehouse; the rest went to the salt driers.

There were two driers, each consisting of a vertical cylindrical drum, about 30 feet tall and 5 feet in diameter, containing a number of horizontal discs, about 2 feet apart, spinning about a vertical axle. Between the discs were fixed shelves sloping down from the sides of the cylinder. Undried salt entered one drum at the top and as it fell it met an upward stream of hot air and was kept moving and circulating by the rotating discs. As it dried it tumbled from disc to shelf alternately until it reached the bottom of the drum, from which it was conveyed to the top of the second drier, which acted as a cooler as the hot dried salt descended through an upward stream of cold air.

The moving of the salt from the filters to the driers and to the warehouses was carried out by four elevators and seven conveyor belts. Pure dried vacuum salt was stored in silos, from which it could be loaded into special bulk-salt road vehicles, and from these it could be discharged through flexible hoses, by compressed air, into storage silos on commercial customers' premises. Other dried salt was conveyed to a bagging plant controlled by three men who could bag and load up to 200 tons in a day. Packaging machines had been installed on the top floor of the dried-salt warehouse but they were never used. In the undried warehouse was a large travelling crane with a grab which could lift 2½ tons of loose salt at a time into lorries or rail wagons or into a hopper to feed the undried bagging plant in the same building.

The vacuum plant was highly mechanised, the processes were monitored with much instrumentation, and there was a laboratory for testing the quality of the brine used and the salt produced. When the Stoke plant was commissioned in 1950, the other vacuum plants already existing at Winsford and Weston Point were only producing a dense fine salt with grains of regular cubic structure. Research and trials at Stoke with the Krystal Oslo evaporators pioneered the new product, granular salt, to replace open-pan coarse salt. Another new product, dendritic salt, was developed by ICI at about the same time. This is formed by a patent process involving the introduction of about fifty parts in a million of sodium, or potassium, ferrocyanide into the brine used for making fine salt, which causes the evaporation process to produce distorted feathery crystals of low-bulk-density salt which is less liable to cake and is more easy to handle than normal vacuuum salt, and is in demand, especially for export. Dendritic salt was not produced commercially at Stoke, but was sent down from Winsford in bags for distribution locally.

Of greater impact on the industry was the discovery that the caking tendency of normal vacuum salt can be prevented by spraying it, whilst on the conveyer belt, with sodium ferrocyanide solution so that the final product contains only four parts per million of ferrocyanide. This process was introduced at the Stoke vacuum plant by the mid 1950s and made possible the use of bulk-salt vehicles to carry, and pneumatic means to discharge, pure dried vacuum salt. Equipment and methods tested at Stoke in the early 1950s were soon incorporated into modernised and replacement plants at Weston Point and Winsford respectively.

In the Stoke vacuum plant the succession of heat exchanges in the evaporators helped to achieve a great economy in fuel, about 20 per cent of that needed to produce the same amount of salt by the open-pan method. There was also a great economy of labour, for whereas a fine-salt open pan, with four men (three salt makers and a lofter) produced about 42 tons per week, the vacuum method, with four teams of five men, produced up to 2,500 tons per week — more than ten times as much per man. However, the vacuum plant did require a very large capital outlay and a back-up team of mechanical and electrical engineers, so it was essential to maintain maximum output and efficiency to recoup the capital costs and to be profitable. In the years before its closure the Stoke vacuum plant, with an output of some 145,000 tons per annum, was supplying about 10 per cent of UK salt production.

End of open-pan salt production

As initial problems were solved and production at the Stoke Works vacuum plant proved successful and reliable, the remaining open pans of the works began to be run down. The six broad-salt pans in B6 panhouse between the vacuum plant and the works railway bridge continued in production for some time, as did many of the open pans to the east of the canal. The machine pans were done away with and the panhouse demolished in 1952. Eventually just sufficient of the open pans were kept going to supply the old mill. An aerial photograph in the *Bromsgrove Messenger* of 28 July 1956, but taken sometime earlier, shows the North Row fine-salt panhouses and the 'Infirmary' broad-salt panhouse still standing, but others had disappeared. Open-pan salt production finally came to an end in July 1956. During the following months buildings were demolished and the site cleared on the east side of the canal. Demolition of the big chimney, which had not been used for almost four years, was started in August 1956. It took steeplejacks and others about nine months to dismantle. Its disappearance marked the end of the centuries-old open-pan method of salt production at Stoke which had provided employment for some

500 or more people in the area in its heyday. The site was sold to Messrs Sto-Chem (later Uni-Royal) who set up a chemical plant, opened in the summer of 1962, to make synthetic rubber latex from the waste residue of crude oil.

Demise of the works railways and rail transport

Another casualty of circumstances and 'progress' was the end of the use of railway transport for bringing in coal and distributing salt. When the Salt Union acquired the vans and wagons of John Corbett in 1889, they were soon repainted to show Salt Union ownership. An existing record book kept from 1892 to 1894 by George Honeybourne, wagon-weigher, lists some 245 wagons and 350 vans then in use, built and maintained in the Stoke Works van shop. For many years there was a daily departure of trains from the works sidings. One northwards through Bromsgrove to Washwood Heath marshalling yard, known as the 'Salto', comprised empty coal wagons, salt vans and wagons, and also repaired wagons picked up from the Bromsgrove Wagon Works. It left at about 4.00 pm. Other trains took salt to the south and west of England and Wales, some to Fishguard for export to Ireland. The distribution of salt by rail from Stoke came to an end in about 1965 with the closure of Bromsgrove Wagon Works in 1964 and the impending closure of Stoke Works Station in 1966.

Over the years the railway system within the works played a vital role in the moving of coal to the many furnaces of the panhouses and in allowing salt to be loaded under cover from the mills and warehouses and directly from alongside the stoves. Horses were long retained and stabled at the works for hauling individual wagons of coal or vans of salt to and from locations remote from the main sidings. This continued into the 1950s, the last stableman being Joe Bloomfield. For many years Corbett's four-wheel steam locomotives *Elephant* and *Raven* continued to shunt vans and wagons around the works' sidings. Each needed to be overhauled and its boiler repaired every few years. *Elephant* (built by P W Hawthorne-Leslie of Newcastle-upon-Tyne) worked mainly on the west side of the canal and was driven and cared for by Gus Harrison for many years; he kept her oiled and polished and in superb condition. *Raven* (a product of the Boyne Engineering Works, Leeds) worked chiefly on the east side and for many years her driver was George ('Billy Harry') Nicklin. Both these locos were still in use in the early 1920s, and *Elephant* remained until after World War Two, having by then been joined by *Worcester*. In May 1913 another four-wheel engine *Annie* arrived from Cheshire and was driven by Bill Harrison. When the Droitwich Covercroft Salt Works closed in 1922, its locomotive *Avon*, a six-wheeler, came to Stoke Works but, in spite of the flanges being removed from the two middle wheels, it could not easily negotiate the sharp 50-feet radius curves and was soon dispatched to Winsford. Its driver was Harry Holden. Two other 0-4-0 locomotives which appeared in later years were *Newbridge* from Winsford, driven by George Taylor, and *Vengeance*. Around 1960 ICI replaced the remaining works' steam locomotives by two 88 h.p. Ruston-Hornsby diesels. The drivers of these worked two shifts, 6 am to 2 pm and 2 pm to 10 pm.

The locomotive Elephant *and Salt Union wagons on the west side of the works.*

Loading Salt Union rail vans with packets of cut lumps inside the works.

Closure of the works

Around 1970 the Droitwich Rural District Council and the Worcestershire County Council were pressing the ICI to stop pumping brine and to close the works because of the fear of further subsidence in the Droitwich area, where a new housing estate was planned. The extent of the danger was uncertain, but whereas in the old days it would have been well nigh impossible to lay the blame for subsidence upon any one of several salt producers in Droitwich and Stoke, now ICI would have been legally liable and could have been faced with costly litigation and heavy penalties. So ICI agreed to close the works in 1973; but in October 1971 it was announced that closure would be brought forward to March 1972. However, in January 1972 a national strike of coal miners began which lasted nine weeks. Long before the strike ended all the coal stocks at the vacuum plant were exhausted and the works ceased producing salt at midnight on 15 February 1972. In the following months enough men were retained to oversee and carry out the dismantling of the plant. Much of it was scrapped, but the closed-type Krystal Oslo evaporator no. 3A survived and was incorporated into the Weston Point vacuum plant. The three brine pits, situated across the canal, were filled in, using 500 tons of limestone, in the late autumn of 1972. When Imperial Row was demolished about this time, an old brine well was located in the garden of no. 1, close to the railway embankment. About 3 feet in diameter, lined with bricks inside a liner of sheet lead, 180 feet deep but with the brine level about 100 feet below the surface, this pit was the original brine source on the west side of the canal and served the Imperial Works. It had long been covered over with a cast-iron plate and topped with concrete slabs. It was filled in on 5 July 1973 with some 75 tons of limestone and capped with concrete.

During the almost twenty-two years of its operation, the vacuum plant had been run with between seventy and eighty employees whose working conditions were much more congenial than those which had been endured by the open-pan salt makers and salt drawers. The last two general managers were Tom Moffatt, who served from 1953 to 1965 and whose involvement with the social and sporting events at Stoke Works was widely appreciated, and Alan Shaw, who served for seven years and had the painful job of supervising the closure and demolition of the highly successful vacuum plant.

Thus came to an end 147 years of salt industry at Stoke Prior. The chemical industry, which had already replaced it on the east side of the canal, soon also extended to the west side, taking over the offices of the ICI across the Hanbury Road, and becoming a subsidiary of Bayer UK.

By 1967 the Bromsgrove Urban District Council had decided to demolish Sagebury Terrace which they bought from the ICI and to replace it with modern houses. Demolition took place over the next six years as tenants moved out and were mostly rehoused locally. Shrubbery Terrace was also pulled down to create an open space between Shaw Lane and the canal. With most of the houses provided for the workers in the nineteenth century pulled down and shops closed, the close-knit community of Stoke Works, where many families had been neighbours for years, has lost a great deal of its character as an industrial village.

Of the salt works itself, little remains to be seen of the once widespread industrial complex. It is to be hoped that the fragments that remain will be preserved to kindle the interest of future generations in the salt industry which existed there for so long. These fragments include the bridge that carried the railway over the canal; the entrance to the old canal arm under the canal towpath and part of the tunnel that existed under the former BAC salt works; bricked-up arches through which coal was supplied from canal boats to fuel the boilers of the steam-pumping engines; the foreman's house close to the site of the large no. 3 brine well; and the large brine reservoir on the hillside, now used to store fresh water for the Bayer chemical works. In addition, the three local former homes of John Corbett still stand, Rigby Hall, Stoke Grange and Chateau Impney, now used respectively by a computer software business, by an educational trust, and as a spectacular hotel.

Appendix A: Apprenticeship indenture, 1869

The following indenture, or legal agreement, for the seven-year apprenticeship of fourteen-year-old Joseph Spalding of Stoke Prior is of social interest on account of the conditions imposed upon both the employer, John Corbett, and the lad, and also because of the involvement of the local church and charity. It occurs in an Agreements Ledger containing copies of many commercial and other agreements entered into by John Corbett in the 1860s and 1870s which is now in the keeping of the Salt Museum, Northwich, Cheshire. Amongst these agreements is one in 1872 with the postmaster general for a telegraph line and apparatus linking Stoke Works with the post office in Bromsgrove; one in 1877 with Corbett's agents in Bristol in which they undertake to transfer from the narrow- to the broad-gauge consignments of salt sent by rail; and one authorising a London firm to be the sole purveyor of salt to the English Refreshment Department at the Paris Universal Exhibition of 1878.

> This Indenture made the tenth day of November One thousand eight hundred & sixty nine — Between Joseph Spalding of the parish of Stoke Prior in the county of Worcester (who was the age of fourteen years on the first day of July last) son of John Spalding of the same place Painter & Glazier of the first part, John Corbett of Stoke Works in the same parish and County Salt Manufacturer of the second part, and the Reverend Francis John Bodfield Hooper, Rector of the parish of Upton Warren in the same county, and Joseph Partridge and John Lees the churchwardens for the time being of the said parish of the third part. Witnesseth that the said Joseph Spalding doth put himself apprentice to the said John Corbett to learn the art of a Painter & Glazier and with him after the manner of an Apprentice to serve as from the first day of July as now past until the first day of July One Thousand eight hundred and seventy six. During which term the said apprentice his master faithfully shall serve, his secrets keep, his lawful commands everywhere gladly do, he shall do no damage to the said master, nor see to be done to others, but to his power shall tell or forthwith give warning to his said master of the same, he shall not waste the goods of the said Master nor lend them unlawfully to any, he shall not commit fornication nor contract matrimony within the said term, he shall not play at cards or dice tables or other unlawful games whereby his master may have any loss with his own goods or others during the said term, without license of his said master he shall neither buy nor sell, he shall not haunt Taverns or Playhouses nor absent himself from his said Master's service day or night unlawfully — But in all things as a faithful apprentice he shall behave himself towards his Master and all his during the said term.
>   And the said John Corbett in consideration of the premises and of the sum of Ten pounds to him paid by the said Rector and Churchwardens of Upton Warren out of the funds of a public Charity, known as Charity for apprenticing poor boys resident in the parishes of Upton Warren, Stoke Prior and Chaddesley Corbett, Doth hereby covenant with the said Francis John Bodfield Hooper, Joseph Partridge and John Lees and also as a separate and distinct covenant with the said Joseph Spalding his apprentice that he his said apprentice in the art of a Painter & Glazier which in his trade and by his servants he useth by the best

means that he can shall cause to be taught and instructed and also that he the said John Corbett shall during the continuance of the said term in lieu of finding unto his said apprentice meat drink lodgings Tools or any other necessaries pay unto his said apprentice weekly wages after the rates hereinafter mentioned that is to say until the first day of July One thousand eight hundred and seventy after the rate of seven shillings per week from the first day of July One thousand eight hundred and seventy during the next year eight shillings per week and from the first day of July One thousand eight hundred and seventy one during the next year nine shillings per week and from the first day of July One thousand eight hundred and seventy two during the next year ten shillings per week and from the first day of July One thousand eight hundred and seventy three eleven shillings per week and from the first day of July One thousand eight hundred and seventy four during the next year twelve shillings per week and from the first day of July One thousand eight hundred and seventy five during the next year thirteen shillings per week — And for the true performance of all end every the said covenants and agreements each and every of the said parties bindeth himself unto the other and others by these presents. In Witness whereof the parties above named to these Indentures interchangeably have put their hands and seals the tenth day of November and in the Thirty third year of the Reign of our Sovereign Lady Victoria by the Grace of God of the United Kingdom of Great Britain and Ireland Queen Defender of the Faith and in the year of our Lord One Thousand Eight hundred and sixty nine.

    Signed sealed & delivered   Joseph Spalding
    by the said Joseph Spalding
    in the presence of Joseph Parkes, clerk to Mr E Housman
        Solicitor Bromsgrove
    signed sealed & delivered   John Corbett
    by the said John Corbett, in the presence of H S Polson.

Appendix B: 'George's Ghost'

George Denning Bate spent practically the whole of his working life as a carpenter and latterly foreman carpenter based at Tardebigge New Wharf Depot on the Worcester and Birmingham Canal. However, on leaving school at the age of thirteen in 1914 he spent about a year working in the salt works which was not far from his canalside home at Stoke Pound. The following experience of his, described in the November 1969 issue of *Fifty-Eight*, the magazine of the Worcester and Birmingham Canal Society, relates to the long brick-arched tunnel arm in which boats were loaded from the old fine-salt panhouses of the North Row and the Bell Row, as well as from the old mill at the far end of the arm.

> This happened when I had just started to work at the Salt Union's Stoke Prior salt works in October 1914. The mill foreman, a Mr.J.Barker, collected me to do a job. He said, "Come along with me; I have a job for you". He took me to the centre of the mill where there were railway metals with rail vans here and there being loaded with salt. There was one space clear where men were removing planks from between the rails; two men then set a plank in position down into a dark hole. This plank I noticed was highly polished with constant friction. Mr. Barker said to me "Get on that plank and slide down". Now I did not question why, I did as I was told, very uneasy in mind as I slid down. Then suddenly I saw a shadowy figure in white moving about in the gloom, appearing to be suspended in space at the time. I was just about to lose control of my bowel movement when this figure spoke to me. "Well George, have they sent you down to help me?" I quickly recovered my composure when I recognised the voice. It was Mr.D.Merrell. He was stood in a canal boat and the boat was in the canal tunnel that runs under the salt works, which I did not know existed at that time. He had been part loading the boat with salt lower down the tunnel and his clothing was lightly covered with salt dust, and the only light he had got was a vessel like a coffee pot with a wick down the spout into the oil. There were a lot of these vessels used at that time; the ones I have seen were mostly made of copper. However, it did not give much of a light. The job I had to do was to take the parcels of cut lumps off the plank as they slid down to me and hand them on to Mr.Merrell to stack in the boat. I did not go back up that plank when I had finished the job; I went out of the tunnel in the boat into the main canal that runs through these works. The boat was Henry Johnson's, Holt St. Wharf, Birmingham, named the "Medway", one of the two boats that Mr.Merrell worked with his wife, and later on with his two sons Jack and Dennis, to Birmingham, two trips every week.

Appendix C: Stoke Works Village

The following description of Stoke Works village is compiled almost verbatim from the typescript of lectures given to various organisations by the late Alf Nicklin in the 1960s. Alf was foreman in the open-pan salt works. He lived in the Brine Pump House (still standing) and took a great interest in the history both of the works and the village:

> Stoke Works has been described as the most sombre village in Worcestershire. John Corbett was content for his workers to live in the continual pollution caused by the poisonous smoke spewed out from his sixty or more chimneys. Babies had to be brought indoors several times a day to have their tiny nostrils cleared of soot; and the re-rinsing of clothes hung out to dry was a regular feature of wash day. If there was any colour at all in this drab village it was brought by the boaties. Their boats were gaily decorated with simple scenes painted in the most vivid colours. There were rarely fewer than twenty boats tied up, waiting to load. During these idle periods the boaties shopped in the two village shops. The bigger one, Hope's, was run by Miss Hope, the daughter of the original owner. It was a general store and post office and was taken over in 1912 by J B Wilson & Sons. At Wilson's Miss Marjorie Honeybourne was the post mistress for many years. The other little shop was at the corner by the canal bridge and was kept by a lovely old lady, Mrs Moore, who always wore a black dress and a lace cap, and was the daughter of the original shop owner. Oh, the delectable aroma of that little shop; tobacco, beans, bacon, black pudding and sweets together. Here one could get a pennyworth of bread pudding cut from the tin or the most savoury faggots scooped up with a spoon.
>
> Before World War One, immediately on the east side of the Boat Bridge there used to be a near derelict building divided into two sections. George and Bert Stanworth worked in the section nearest the bridge. They were blacksmiths and farriers. The other part of the building was occupied by a long established business belonging to Thomas Weaver who was a wheelwright and also the local undertaker. Mr Weaver would convey coffins to a bereaved household, using his tricycle as a handcart. Along Shaw Lane on the west side there used to be a sawmill. Up to about 1900 it was run by George Gibbons who supplied the wooden shingles for the elegant spire of Stoke Prior Church. Then, until about 1930, it was worked by Charles Gittus. He owned a steam traction engine which was used to haul a huge timber wagon. Another well-known and much loved character was Ikey Weetman, the village cobbler, who was wholly deaf and dumb.
>
> Life in Stoke Works for the families of salt workers in the nineteenth century and the early years of the twentieth was never easy. As elsewhere, families were large, with as many as ten or more children. There was no immunisation against measles, polio, scarlet fever, whooping cough and diphtheria, and epidemics of these caused many deaths. To help families afflicted by illness and bereavement, there were at each of the three village pubs, The Boat and Railway, the Butchers Arms and the Bowling Green, sick and dividend clubs. Members paid a small weekly contribution in return for payments in times of sickness and inability to work, any accumulated surplus being paid out as a Christmas dividend. Also, for over fifty years, some of the wives ran a death and dividend club, insuring families against death in the sum of £5, with, again, any surplus paid out as dividend at

Christmas.

Perhaps the best known institution in Stoke Works was The Bull, the works steam hooter. It controlled the lives of people in, and far beyond, the village. At 5.40 am it produced two deafening blasts to rouse the sleepy worker, and another single one at 6.00 am, when he was due to start work. It sounded at lunchtime and then at 6.00 pm (latterly 5.30 pm) to signal the end of the working day for non-shift workers. The Bull was also sounded to signal joyous events like coronations and jubilees, as an alarm in case of fire at the works, and in wartime to warn of air raids. It blew for the last time on Friday 30 June 1950.

Some documentary sources

In the Public Record Office, Kew
  Worcester and Birmingham Canal Company Committee Minutes, Ref. Rail:886.

In Worcester Record Office (St Helen's branch)
  Papers relating to Francis Rufford and the British Alkali Company. Ref. 705:260.
  Many deeds, agreements and other documents relating to the lease and purchase of land for the salt works and other properties and estates in the ownership of John Corbett, from the offices of Messrs Vizard, solicitors. Ref. 705:35.
  John Corbett's business letters, 1870-78. Ref. 899:1029.
  Salt Union Stoke Prior Letter Book August 1894 to February 1900. Ref. 899:1029.
  Agreements and other documents concerning John Corbett and the Salt Union from Droitwich Borough Archives. Ref. 261:4.

In Birmingham Central Reference Library
  Birmingham Urban Sanitary Authority, Register of Canal Boats from 1879.

In the Salt Museum, Northwich, Cheshire
  Agreements ledger containing copies of many of John Corbett's business agreements, 1856-78.
  An inventory of Salt Union properties, 1908.
  Various museum publications about the salt industry, trade associations and the Salt Union.
  Part of an unpublished draft history of the ICI Salt Division, by W G Kerwin.

Books and pamphlets
  The Salt Springs of Worcestershire, a lecture by Charles Hastings, MD, FGS to Worcestershire Natural History Society, 1835. (Sir Charles Hastings was a Worcester physician who founded what became the BMA.)
  A History of the Chemical Industry in Widnes by D W F Hardie, 1950. (Refers to Gossage's career and work at Stoke Prior.)
  The Manufacturing Industries of Worcestershire by W D Curzon, 1881.
  Trade Directories of Worcestershire in Worcester City Library and Bromsgrove Public Library
  The Story of Salt ICI Mond Division Information Service, 1966.
  Soap-Making at Stoke Works, Bromsgrove, and its connection with the Salt-Making Industry there by B C G Nokes, 1959.
  A History of the Salt Union by A F Calvert, 1913.
  Stoke Schools Centenary Souvenir Brochure, 1972.
  'Farrin's Boatyard' by Alan White in *Fifty-Eight* (the magazine of the Worcester and Birmingham Canal Society), April 1986.